WATERSIDE WALKS

In Leicestershire & Rutland

Other areas covered in the Waterside Walks series include:

Berkshire

Bristol & Bath

Cheshire

The Cotswolds

Derbyshire

Devon

Dorset

Essex

Hampshire

Kent

Lancashire

Lincolnshire

Middlesex & West London

Norfolk

Northamptonshire

Nottinghamshire

Oxfordshire

Shropshire

Somerset

Staffordshire

Suffolk

Surrey

Sussex

Warwickshire

Worcestershire

Yorkshire

WATERSIDE WALKS
In Leicestershire & Rutland

Bryan Waites

COUNTRYSIDE BOOKS
NEWBURY, BERKSHIRE

First published 2000
© Bryan Waites 2000

COUNTRYSIDE BOOKS
3 Catherine Road
Newbury, Berkshire

To view our complete range of books,
please visit us at
www.countrysidebooks.co.uk

ISBN 1 85306 608 7

Designed by Graham Whiteman
Cover illustration by Colin Doggett
Maps by the author
Photographs by Beryl Waites

Produced through MRM Associates Ltd., Reading
Typeset by Hardlines, Charlbury, Oxford
Printed by Woolnough Bookbinding Ltd, Irthlingborough

Contents

Introduction

Walk

AREA MAP SHOWING LOCATION OF THE WALKS

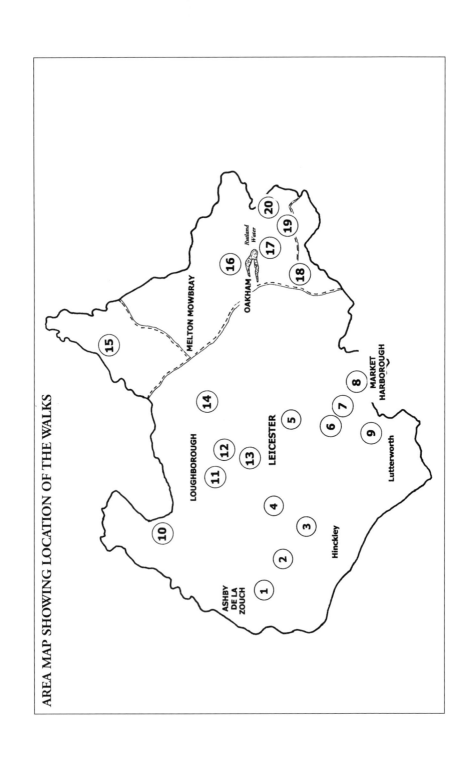

Walk

✦✦✦

For Melissa, Camilla, Brittany, Oliver, Ryan, Natalie, Olivia

PUBLISHER'S NOTE

We hope that you obtain considerable enjoyment from this book; great care has been taken in its preparation. Although at the time of publication all routes followed public rights of way or permitted paths, diversion orders can be made and permissions withdrawn.

We cannot, of course, be held responsible for such diversion orders and any inaccuracies in the text which result from these or any other changes to the routes nor any damage which might result from walkers trespassing on private property. We are anxious though that all details covering the walks are kept up to date and would therefore welcome information from readers which would be relevant to future editions.

INTRODUCTION

Waterside walking holds an appeal for all ages. It is an ever-available source of outdoor recreation and provides constant interest along the way - colourful narrowboats negotiating canal locks, fishermen patiently awaiting their day's catch and, everywhere, water-loving birds and other wildlife.

Although Leicestershire has no coastline, it is possible to seek out walks beside water in all areas and I have enjoyed putting together this collection of 20 routes which include every type of waterway to be found.

The Soar and the Welland are Leicestershire's two main rivers and, while there are few natural lakes, several man-made reservoirs are now blending into the landscape. The Grand Union Canal traverses the county and there are a number of smaller canals in various stages of preservation, such as the Ashby and Grantham Canals.

In the old coal mining regions of the north-west there are flashes (small lakes) caused by land subsidence, and in some riverine areas, such as Watermead and Cossington, there are man-made lakes which are the remnants of gravel extraction.

Rutland has only a few minor streams but over three per cent of its surface area is covered by Rutland Water and Eyebrook Reservoir, providing waterside walks galore!

Fortunately, Leicestershire County Council's 'Waymark 2000 Project', in association with the Countryside Commission, has succeeded in signposting 3,000 miles of footpaths and public rights of way. Now the walker can be assured of finding the route and seeing it clearly. In particular, the improved public access may draw attention to lovely walks which otherwise could remain undiscovered.

Much of the walking is level and easy - particularly when along the canal towpaths - but it is wise to wear boots or stout footwear. You should, of course, always be careful near the waterside, especially when you are with children.

The walks are circular and vary between 2 miles and $5\frac{1}{2}$ miles, suitable for all members of the family. Along the way or at the beginning or end there will be a pub, hotel or tearoom where you can have refreshment. When you park your car please make sure it does not impede or annoy local people. If you want to leave your car in the pub car park while you are walking, please obtain the permission of the landlord first. Telephone numbers have been given so that you can check opening times and menus in advance, if you wish.

If you are having a day out you may want to combine walks. For example, Walk 1 is short. You could do this in the morning then go on to Walk 2, only a few miles away, have lunch at the excellent Globe Inn alongside the canal and then complete the second walk. You may even have time to travel on the Battlefield Line and back – all in a day! So, have a good look at the walks available and work out how you intend to do them – there is a series quite close together, for example, along the Grand Union Canal.

Also helping to extend your family day out is the section 'Places of Interest Nearby'. I have tried to include a good selection of Leicestershire and Rutland's attractions, arranged with regard to their proximity to each walk.

The sketch maps should be adequate to follow the route but they are not to scale. Therefore you may wish to have an Ordnance Survey map with you – these are particularly useful for identifying the main features or views. I have given the number of the relevant OS Landranger or (where available) Explorer sheet for each walk. As you go on your way, remember your responsibilities to follow the Countryside Code, respecting both people and environment.

I am grateful for the companionship and advice of Dr Gillian Dawson and Beryl Waites on the walks and to Beryl also for the photographs. We took great pleasure in discovering routes that were new to us. They were a real delight and we were sorry when our task was completed. Better still, the walks did us a power of good both mentally and physically. They reminded us what a wonderful country we live in and how much more there always is for us to get to know.

I hope you also will take the opportunity to find some secret scenery and enjoy the solitude which is so hard to come by in the bustle of everyday life.

Bryan Waites

SALTERSFORD VALLEY: LAKESIDE WALKING IN THE NATIONAL FOREST

*'Not for 1,000 years has a new Forest been created on such a scale.
Here in the heart of England, the National forest is not just a dream,
it is happening.' This lovely waterside walk in the Saltersford Valley is
located in its midst.*

A lake in the Saltersford Valley

The area between Newtown Linford in Charnwood Forest and Hoar Cross in Needwood Forest, a distance of almost 30 miles covering 200 square miles, has been designated the National Forest and 30 million trees, mainly British broadleaves and conifers, are being planted over the whole area, one-third of which will be forest and woodland in future. Once this region was industrial but now much of that industry has gone. The legacy on the landscape, though, can still be seen. One of the most prominent features is land subsidence left by former coal mining. Between Moira, Donisthorpe and Oakthorpe, in north-west Leicestershire, there are many flashes, or lakes, which are due to subsidence. Several of these are in the Saltersford

Valley. This derelict land has been rescued by Leicestershire County Council and landscaped as part of the National Forest. Today the transformation is nearly complete here.

On this site there are 6 acres of woodland with all-weather trails suitable for wheelchair use with assistance. Features include two sculptures, meadowland, lakes and a picnic area, and many walks start from here. Hundreds of local schoolchildren have helped to shape the new woodland by planting trees in a scheme run by Radio 1 and BBC TV.

A short extension of the walk takes you to the Holly Bush Inn in Oakthorpe where you will find a good family pub with traditional cask ales, bottled Continental and English beers, fine wines, bar meals at lunchtime and early evening, freshly cut sandwiches and cobs made to order as well as a Continental and English menu (evenings only). A warm welcome awaits the visitor and there is plenty of room inside. The inn has a big car park and a children's play area. Telephone: 01530 270943.

- **HOW TO GET THERE:**   Make for the A/M42 between Tamworth and Ashby de la Zouch. At junction 12 join the B5006 for Measham. Just after entering Measham you come to a set of traffic lights. Turn right onto the B586 Oakthorpe road. Do not go left into the village but keep on the B586 and in about ½ mile you will see Saltersford Valley Picnic Area on your left.
- **PARKING:** There is a car park at the site (restricted by 2 metre height barrier – minibus drivers must request a key in advance) open from 9 am to 7 pm in the summer and until 4 pm in the winter. Enquiries to Leicestershire County Council (telephone: 01162 657061/657221).
- **LENGTH OF THE WALK:** 2 miles. Map: OS Landranger 128 Derby (GR 325133).

THE WALK

1. Start at the car park. Go through the wooden gate where you will find a map of the site. At the picnic tables turn left through a hand gate. Keep left uphill as the path divides. You are now between two lakes. On your left you will see a gate leading to an area still to be developed. You can go to see this but return to the main path and continue round.

2. Rejoin your original path and on reaching the picnic area again bear left to walk on the jetty, which straddles the lake. Follow this round, diverting to walk on a grass path to your left which takes you alongside a lake.

3. Return to your original path and continue but where the path divides keep straight on to the car park.

4. Now go through the hand gate opposite. At the marker post turn left to follow the path to the main road. Go a little way along the road to a path on your right. This crosses the fields to Oakthorpe.

5. On reaching the village lane turn left to the Holly Bush Inn. Retrace your steps later to return to the car park at Saltersford Valley Picnic Area.

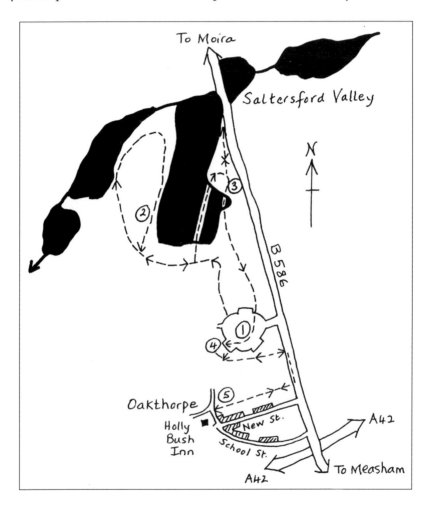

PLACES OF INTEREST NEARBY

Visit the *National Forest Visitor Centre* (telephone: 01283 216633) in Bath Lane on the B5003 in Moira. Parking is free all day and there is a lakeside restaurant. Picnics and packed lunches can be provided. Nearby there is the *Moira Furnace*, an impressive early 19th century blast furnace and craft workshops, also *Donisthorpe Country Park*. *Twycross Zoo* is just a few miles south (telephone: 01827 880250). *Ashby de la Zouch Castle and Museum* and the interesting town are only minutes away. *Measham Museum*, 56 High Street (telephone: 01530 273956) is a small village museum, admission free, but please check the limited opening times.

A pleasant spot for a picnic

THE ASHBY CANAL AND THE BATTLEFIELD LINE

A very pleasant walk for 3 miles along the Ashby de la Zouch Canal brings you to Shackerstone where you can catch the Battlefield Line - the steam railway - to Shenton Station and the Battlefield of Bosworth, with all its attractions. You can make a day of this if you wish and return later to walk back via country lanes and over the fields to Snarestone.

Narrowboats moored on the canal

The Ashby Canal was built between 1794 and 1804. It ran south for 30 miles along the 300 ft contour to join the Coventry Canal at Marston Junction near Nuneaton and it was lock-free except for the stop lock at Marston. The intention had been to link with the River Trent to the north but the canal never reached beyond the Ashby Wolds. By clever use of tramways, coal and other materials were transported to the canal. The Ashby Canal Co was bought out by the Midland Railway in 1845 but traffic still used the canal until the 1940s when, due to subsidence problems, the northern section had to be closed and eventually filled in. Though Snarestone is now the terminus, the course of the canal can still be seen and followed in the Moira/Donisthorpe area, and you will come across the Ashby Canal again if you walk in the Bosworth area.

Both Snarestone and Shackerstone are very interesting villages with 18th century buildings and thatched cottages. In the latter village St Peter's, with its 15th century tower, and the nearby Rising Sun, an attractive, traditional inn (telephone: 01827 880215), together form a lovely scene.

In Snarestone the Globe Inn provides an excellent start to the walk since the canal is next to the pub. There is plenty of space for children, together with a play area and a lovely garden. As well as restaurant meals you will find bar snacks (available all day), among them 12 inch baguettes with chips and salad. Real ales are on offer with Bass Red Label being highlighted, also Theakston Mild, John Smith's Smooth, Worthington Cream Bitter, Guinness on draught, Carling lager and Blackthorn cider, plus various wines. Barbecues are held on Friday, Saturday and Sunday evenings in season. Telephone: 01530 270272.

Snarestone Tunnel

- **HOW TO GET THERE:**   From the M42 leave at junction 11, go south on the A444 and follow signs to Snarestone or from junction 12 drive into Measham and then south to Snarestone. From the A5 join the A444 to Twycross then follow signs. The Globe Inn is in Main Street.

- **PARKING:** There is an excellent car park for customers at the Globe Inn but you must ask the landlord if you want to leave your car there while you are walking. If you prefer, there is some on-street parking.
- **LENGTH OF THE WALK:** 5½ miles. Map: OS Landranger 140 Leicester and Coventry area (GR 344094).

THE WALK

1. Start from the car park of the Globe Inn where you will see a path and steps down to the canal. Turn left to follow the towpath all the way to Bridge 53 at Shackerstone – 3 miles.

2. Go up the steps at the bridge, turn left over the old railway bridge, then left down a country lane at the train sign. Before doing this you may wish to enjoy the fine sight of moored narrowboats from Bridge 53; or to look around Shackerstone; or go to the Battlefield Line and take the train to Shenton and Bosworth Field.

3. To return to Snarestone, continue north-west along the country lane. In 100 yards **do not turn left** but carry straight on for about 1 mile. As the lane bends at Crown Cottage and Jenny's Cattery take the footpath on your left, 'Ivanhoe Way Snarestone 1¼ mile'.

4. Cross the plank bridge and stile then bear right to a marker post in the far left corner of the field. Cross the stile (at the power line) and go through a wood and over the next stile into a field, continuing straight ahead alongside the hedge. After 50 yards cross the stile on your left then turn sharp right alongside the hedge. At a marker post go into the field over a stile then ahead to the far marker post at a stile. Beanfield Farm is to your right.

5. Follow marker posts ahead and at a blue metal gate keep ahead to the next stile (in the trees). Still going ahead, pass through the trees. At the sign 'Ivanhoe Way Public Footpath' turn left for 30 yards to the next signpost, 'Ivanhoe Way Snarestone ½ mile'.

6. Go over the plank bridge into the field. Follow the hedge ahead. Bear left to continue around the edge of the field. Snarestone is now in view ahead. Follow marker posts to the village. At the final stile go diagonally left to the corner of the field, over the stile and into the village lane. Turn right for the main road then left to go back to the Globe Inn.

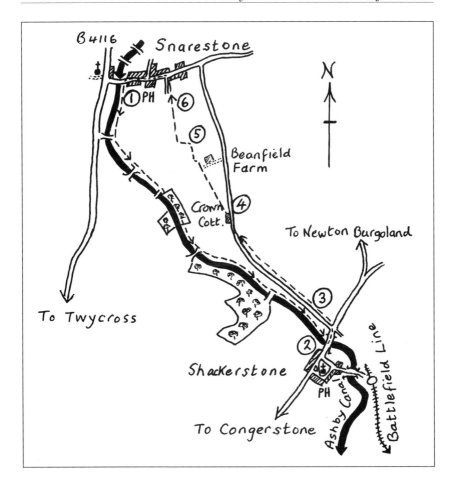

PLACES OF INTEREST NEARBY

The Battlefield Line – a steam-hauled 9 mile round trip from Shackerstone Station, also museum and locos plus tearoom (telephone: 01827 880754). The train will take you to Shenton Station and from there you can visit (from April to October) *Bosworth Battlefield Visitor Centre* with its film theatre, book and gift shop, tourist information, picnic areas, battle trails and special medieval events (for opening times telephone: 01455 290429). *Donington le Heath Manor House*, a superbly restored medieval manor with fine oak furnishings and a herb garden is just south of Coalville. Open daily 11 am to 5 pm (3 pm October to March), free admission (telephone: 01530 831259). *Twycross Zoo* is on the A444 to the south-west of Snarestone (telephone: 01827 880250).

THE BATTLE OF BOSWORTH AND THE ASHBY CANAL

This walk includes a battle trail, traverses Ambion Wood, reaches the Ashby Canal at Sutton Cheney Wharf, then follows the towpath eventually turning to pass the place where King Richard fell in 1485 and ending, as it began, at Shenton Station on the steam-hauled Battlefield Line.

Sutton Cheney Wharf

Would you like to relive a great medieval battle and, in the imagination, thrill to the charge of a body of knights in full armour with their king at their head? This is possible at Bosworth Field where an award-winning recreation of the events of 22nd August 1485 has been successfully accomplished by means of trails, displays, films and models. Bosworth was a major turning point in English history ranking with Hastings and the Battle of Britain. It changed a dynasty and ended the Wars of the Roses by establishing the Tudors on the throne.

Battlefield, canal, railway (see also Walk 2) and not far away the historic town of Market Bosworth comprise an unbeatable formula for a day out.

Added to this is the beauty and charm of the west Leicestershire countryside, often missed by the busy tourist hurrying along the impersonal motorways which skirt the area.

The delightful Battlefield Buttery (licensed) is near the Visitor Centre and serves a variety of hot and cold home-cooked meals, sandwiches, cakes and scones. Vegetarian meals are also available. There are specials boards and you will be offered dishes such as Battlefield Beef Ale Pie, deep fried plaice and roast chicken breast. Open daily between 1st April and 31st October from 10 am to 5 pm. You can eat either inside or at the tables provided outside – a very pleasant setting on fine days. Telephone: 01455 291048.

Off the main route of the walk, about 1 mile away in Sutton Cheney village there are two pubs – the Hercules Inn (telephone: 01455 292591)

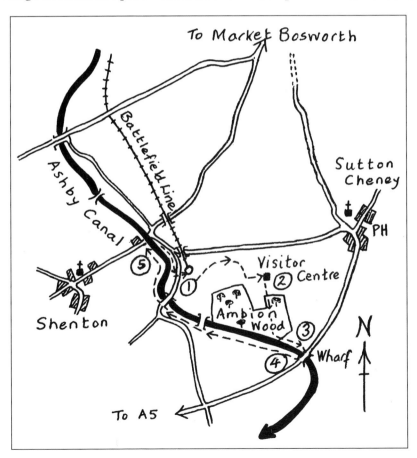

and the Royal Arms (telephone: 01455 290263) – both open daily for meals (not on Mondays or Sunday evenings at the Hercules). Also in the village is the Almshouse (telephone: 01455 291050) which is open daily from 10 am to 6 pm, except on Mondays in winter, and serves morning coffee, afternoon tea, lunches and traditional Sunday lunch (for which booking is essential). Sutton Cheney church is where King Richard prayed the night before the battle.

- **HOW TO GET THERE:**   From the A5 near Atherstone take the Roman road to Fenny Drayton which, in about 6 miles, leads you to Sutton Cheney and the battlefield. This may be the approach road taken by the future King Henry VII. Turn off northwards for Shenton Station before reaching the village. If you are approaching from Market Bosworth or the B585 – or from the A447 – follow signs for Shenton Station.
- **PARKING:**   The walk starts at Shenton Station where there is a large car park and toilets. There is a small charge.
- **LENGTH OF THE WALK:**   3½ miles. Map: OS Landranger 140 Leicester and Coventry area (GR 397004).

The Battlefield Buttery and entrance to the Visitor Centre

THE WALK

1. Cross the railway line at Shenton Station. Turn left uphill then follow the signs 'Battlefield Visitor Centre' to the left. Pass through two gates and bear right uphill, then go through the gate at the top. Carry on along the path then turn right, keeping to the path at King Richard's standard. You reach the Battlefield car park and picnic area. Turn left for the Visitor Centre and the other facilities.

2. Once you have had time to look around (summer months), come out of the Visitor Centre and, with your back to it, you will see a sign 'Sutton Cheney Wharf'. Follow this to the left through a gate (arrow) and continue via a gate into Ambion Wood. This is Path 3 and is well signposted (please keep to the path). You reach the Ashby Canal and continue with it on your right to Sutton Cheney Wharf, usually busy with activity.

3. Now you must find a stile which takes you onto the road and over Bridge 34 to return along the towpath on the other side. At the sign 'Bosworth Battlefield 1 m' turn right onto the towpath.

4. You will walk along this lovely towpath for about $1\frac{3}{4}$ miles, passing under a former railway bridge and then under a road bridge. Here, if you wish, you can go onto the road and turn right to return to Shenton Station which is about $\frac{1}{4}$ mile away. However, it is a very pleasant walk to continue along the towpath for $\frac{1}{4}$ mile to reach the aqueduct.

5. When you see the sign 'Shenton Village' go down the steps on your left and under the aqueduct. Then turn right along the road signposted 'Sutton Cheney $1\frac{3}{4}$'. Follow signs to Shenton Station, bearing right. You pass King Richard's Field where a stone marks the spot where he is believed to have been killed. This is a pleasant picnic park and if you go up the slope you will again see the canal. Return to the main road and then back to Shenton Station.

PLACES OF INTEREST NEARBY
Bosworth Battlefield Visitor Centre is open from early April to the end of October and there are many special events (for opening times telephone: 01455 290429). *Market Bosworth* is a very attractive and historic town. Nearby, on the B585, is *Bosworth Water Trust Leisure and Water Park*, open daily all year from 10 am to dusk. There is a charge per car (telephone: 01455 291876). *Whitemoors Antiques and Craft Centre* is at Shenton (telephone: 01455 212250). The *Battlefield Line* runs from Shenton Station to Shackerstone and, of course, you can actually arrive by train for this walk (telephone: 01827 880754).

AROUND THORNTON RESERVOIR

This is an entirely man-made scene - church, village, dam, reservoir - yet it has all the beauty that Nature might provide. An excellent pathway takes you around the edge of Thornton Reservoir, with fishermen to see most days. Who would guess that such a tranquil place is only a mile away from the M1?

Geese at Thornton Reservoir

A series of reservoirs was established around Charnwood Forest in the latter part of the 19th century - Thornton, Blackbrook, Cropston and Swithland - all attractive and, at the time, supplying water to the city of Leicester. Thornton Reservoir was built in 1854 and is one of the oldest in the county. It now supplies water to homes in Hinckley and elsewhere and lies within the National Forest (see Walk 1). In 1997, the Severn Trent Water Authority and the local council combined to improve access, providing seats, picnic tables, parking, good pathways, woodland walks and fishing facilities. The lovely landscape of Charnwood Forest is a short distance to the east.

The village of Thornton is linear and there are a few old houses and a unique church. Its situation alongside such an attractive lake enhances its appeal. St Peter's is the main landmark. It is unrestored in fabric and furnishings with 'discoveries every foot or so'. These include a great medieval door, perhaps from Ulverscroft Priory, medieval wall-paintings and glass, a chancel screen with original colouring, a complete set of bench ends from around 1560 and a tympanum with the Ten Commandments.

The Tipsy Fisherman pub, formerly the Bull's Head, is just a few minutes walk from the reservoir. The eating and drinking areas are spacious and attractive with some real atmosphere. As well as an interesting menu of main dishes, available both lunchtimes and evenings, there is a good selection of sandwiches and bar snacks, also a children's menu and provision for vegetarians. One unusual feature is the Coffee Menu which has several varieties to choose from. As for drinks, you will find Pedigree, Bass Red Label, Tetley, Caffrey's, Ansell Mild and guest beers supported by Stella, Carling and Carlsberg lager and Strongbow cider. Parking is excellent and there is a patio garden. Telephone: 01530 230287.

- **HOW TO GET THERE:** From the A50 turn off at Field Head, following signs to Thornton (3 miles). From the M1 at junction 22 follow signs to the A50 and Markfield and thence to Thornton.
- **PARKING:** There is a layby for about ten cars at the southern end of the reservoir. At the western end there is the official car park, the gates of which open at 7.30 am and close at 9 pm. You can start the walk from either parking place – the route is clear from both.

Fisherman's Lodge

• **LENGTH OF THE WALK:** 2½ miles. Map: OS Landranger 140 Leicester and Coventry area (layby GR 476072).

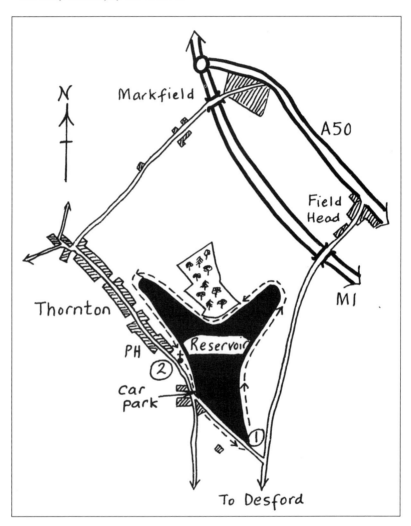

THE WALK

1. I chose to park in the layby. If this is your starting point, go through the hand gate onto the pathway. The surface is good all the way round. The views towards the church are delightful. As you approach the north side of the reservoir you will come across woodland walks which you can follow if you have the time.

2. As you reach below the church, you pass through a wooden hand gate with the Fisherman's Lodge on your left – shaped like an upturned boat. Follow the path to the main car park and then out of the exit, turning left across the dam road to the layby.

PLACES OF INTEREST NEARBY
Tropical Birdland in Lindridge Lane, Desford is just a few miles south. Over 85 species can be seen and there are walks through aviaries, a chick room, a woodland walk, koi ponds, picnic gardens, a shop and rainforest atmosphere (telephone: 01455 824603). The 100-acre *Snibston Discovery Park* in Ashby Road, Coalville includes an exhibition hall with 'hands-on' experience of Science Alive. Open daily (telephone: 01530 813256). *Kirby Muxloe Castle* to the west of Leicester, is a picturesque ruined fortified manor house dating from 1480 (for details telephone: 0116 275555).

THE GRAND UNION CANAL SOUTH OF LEICESTER

The great urban sprawl of the city of Leicester comes to an end in the south as the River Sence and, close by, the Grand Union Canal, bring it to a halt. River and canal run side by side in lovely countryside with attractive communities like Newton Harcourt, Kilby and the lost village of Wistow adding to a quiet rural scene. Who could guess that this tranquil walk is in the shadow of the city?

A canal lock at Newton Harcourt

The walk begins at Wistow Garden Centre which is on the edge of parkland around Wistow Hall. Opposite is the church of St Wistan who was martyred here in AD 847. 'Wistanstowe' was the holy place of Wistan and may have been a large and important Anglo-Saxon estate.

Charles I and Prince Rupert were at Wistow Hall both before and after the Battle of Naseby. The lovely church, one of the few in the county to retain box pews and a two-decker pulpit, has memorials to Sir Richard Halford (died 1658), keeper of the King's saddles, and Sir Henry Halford (1766–1844). He was the royal physician who helped to identify the remains of Charles I and who also discovered that George III suffered from porphyria and was not mad, as many had thought. The medieval village of Wistow is in the fields nearby.

Wistow Garden Centre has a tearoom and café offering snacks and meals (including vegetarian dishes). In good weather it is delightful to sit outside. An aquatic centre, an artists' studio, a doll's house maker, craft shop, a plant centre and a famous model village called Wistan le Dale are all included in the complex, which is open from 10 am to 5 pm daily, closed on Tuesday. Admission is free. Telephone: 0116 2592009.

The walk passes the church and crosses the fields to the canal. It then follows the towpath for about 1½ miles, part of the route being below Newton Harcourt. Thereafter it crosses the fields to Kilby where you can take refreshment at the Dog and Gun in Main Street (telephone: 0116 2402398). There follows another walk through the fields for 1½ miles, ending with a straight bridleway back to Wistow Garden Centre.

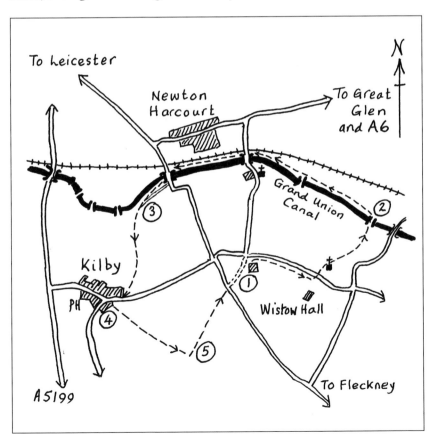

The church of St Wistan

- **HOW TO GET THERE:** From Leicester take either the A6 or the A5199 and in about 6 miles look for signs to Kilby or Wistow. From the M1 leave at junction 21 and follow the A563 to the A5199. Alternatively, leave at junction 20 onto the A4304 then onto the A5199.
- **PARKING:** When open, at Wistow Garden Centre. Otherwise you can park just outside and on rough laybys in the parkland area.
- **LENGTH OF THE WALK:** 5½ miles. Map: OS Landranger 140 Leicester and Coventry area (GR 639959).

THE WALK

1. Start at the Garden Centre car park. Walk to the main entrance. Turn right and walk along the footpath on the main road. When you reach the church you will see a red letter box. Cross here into the footpath, which is signed. Climb the stile, go over the footbridge and follow the path to the next bridge then straight ahead across the field to the stile opposite. Continue ahead alongside the hedge to the corner of the field. Go over the next stile (arrow) and bear left uphill and over the canal bridge. Turn left to join the towpath.

2. Now you walk along the towpath for just over a mile. On the route you pass under Bridges 79 and 80 and then come to Newton Top Lock with the Lock Keeper's Cottage. The next lock is close to Bridge 81. The main road from Wigston to Wistow crosses the canal here. Go under the bridge and turn right to reach the road. Cross the bridge carefully and when you are at the other side you will see a footpath sign on your right. Follow the path between double fences along the canal. At the corner of the field continue in the rough alongside the canal and near a lock. Then the path is in woodland. On emerging from the trees cross through a fence on your left (near a farm building), bear right for about 40 yards to stiles (arrows) which will lead you into rough paddocks. Go ahead to a stile which takes you onto a wide lane.

3. Follow the lane for about 200 yards to a marker post on the left. Keep ahead, passing another marker post, to a stile in the hedge. Then cross the field to the stile opposite. Go over a footbridge then diagonally right under a pylon to a stile in the hedge (arrow). Turn left to a marker post in a dip with houses behind. Here you cross a footbridge then continue uphill to a stile in the hedge at the main road. Cross the road carefully and turn right to walk on the grass verge into Kilby.

4. Where the road bends into Main Street you will see a footpath sign on your left. Follow this through the farmyard between barns to a stile (marker post). Cross into the field and bear right over the large field to the far right corner. Cross the stile here, bearing left to the next marker post and double stile in the hedge. Again cross the next field, bearing slightly right to a gap in the hedge. Cross the stile then continue to the next stile, all well marked with posts and arrows. Finally, you cross the next field towards two close trees and between a marker post. Here you will see the blue arrow for the bridlepath on the opposite side of the post.

5. Turn left to follow a wide grassy path which gives excellent walking for $\frac{1}{2}$ mile. You arrive at a metal gate almost on the main road. Go onto the road and through the metal gate on your left – or over the cattle grid if you prefer. In 20 yards turn right at the bridlepath sign to follow the path beside the trees. In about 200 yards turn right over a cattle grid into Wistow Garden Centre.

PLACES OF INTEREST NEARBY

Leicester city centre, with all its attractions, is only a few miles away. *St Luke's church* in *Newton Harcourt* is close to the walk. Here you will find a probably unique graveyard monument – a miniature church, a memorial to a young boy. Down the A5199 a few miles will bring you to two of Leicestershire's most pleasant villages, *Arnesby* and *Shearsby*, well worth a walk around.

FLECKNEY AND THE GRAND UNION CANAL

The walk starts on the edge of the village, crossing fields to the Grand Union Canal, then along to Kibworth Bridge and beyond, turning back towards Fleckney over typical rolling Leicestershire countryside. You will probably get the chance to watch narrowboats negotiating the locks on your journey - an ever-fascinating sight.

The start of the walk

According to W. G. Hoskins, Fleckney is 'still redolent of the late Victorian industrial revolution'. Not only the village, but the nearby Grand Union Canal reminds us of this. Rather unjustly, Hoskins adds that the village is 'woefully unattractive', the result of the setting up of hosiery or footwear factories one hundred years ago. Yet the village has a strong character and the canal, now much quieter than in its industrial heyday, has a serene beauty which the walker can appreciate.

The Old Crown is conveniently situated at the end of your walk and is most welcoming, with a large and cosy lounge. Outside you will find a beer garden, patio and car park. This is an Everard's house with Tiger, Beacon, Adnams Best Bitter, Caffery's Irish Ale, Guinness on draught, Stella Artois, Carling and Foster's lagers and Woodpecker cider. Morning coffee is served, also hot and cold bar food, mostly home-made, all day on Friday and Saturday, on Sundays from 12 noon to 4 pm and on other days during the usual opening hours. There is a specials board with an excellent choice. Telephone: 0116 2402223.

- **HOW TO GET THERE:**   Fleckney is south of Leicester, close to the A5199. It can also be reached from the A6, being only a few miles west of the Kibworths.
- **PARKING:**   There is a free car park next to the Baptist Church on the main street.
- **LENGTH OF THE WALK:**   3 miles. Map: OS Landranger 141 Kettering, Corby and surrounding area and 140 Leicester and Coventry area are both needed (GR 651934).

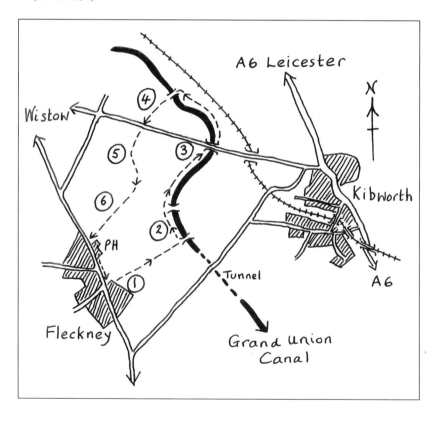

THE WALK

1. Start at the free car park in Fleckney. Turn left into Kibworth Road then first left into a cul-de-sac. Here you see a marker post. Go through a wooden gate and cross the field diagonally right to the left of the canal bridge.

2. Go through a wooden gate to the hedge onto the towpath. Turn left and carry on along the towpath to Kibworth Top Lock via Ross Bridge 74 (which you will go under).

3. You come to the main road bridge (Kibworth Bridge 75) at the third lock. Go through a wooden hand gate then right over the bridge. Now go left onto the towpath to carry on walking to Crane's Lock (Bridge 76). Cross the bridge here. Go over the stile.

4. Carry on to the marker post then through an arable field which at the time of my walk was head high with maize but with a clear path through. You reach a footbridge on the far side. Go ahead to a stile in the far hedge (marker post). Cross a busy main road to the footpath sign opposite. Go to a path at the far left side of this field.

The Grand Union Canal

5. Follow marker posts to cross fields via a footbridge and stiles. Then along the hedge on your right. At the corner go over a stile to your right (marker post) and carry on with the hedge on your left. Power lines and Fleckney are ahead.

6. At the corner cross the stile on your left and go ahead alongside the hedge to a wooden hand gate. Now continue alongside the hedge on your right, under power lines, through a metal gate and straight on to a gateway, then to houses ahead at the main road. Go through a metal gate into the main road and turn left to return to the village centre and the Old Crown.

PLACES OF INTEREST NEARBY

Wistan le Dale Model Village is located at Wistow Garden Centre, just over 1 mile away from Fleckney. This unique model village covers 2,400 square feet within a Georgian walled garden. The garden centre is also of great interest with a café and other attractions (telephone: 0116 2592009). A little to the north, at 42/44 Bushloe End in Wigston there is the *Wigston Framework Knitters' Museum*, a house with a garden workshop unaltered for 60 years and dating from the 18th century. Open on the first Saturday in the month and every Sunday, 2 pm to 5 pm (telephone: 0116 2883396). *Farmworld, Stoughton Farm Park* is on Gartree Road in Oadby, $3\frac{1}{2}$ miles south of the city centre, signposted from the A6 and A47. 'Britain's biggest and brightest working farm park' – shire horses, cart rides, rare farm animals, a working dairy farm, chicken hatchery, lakeside and woodland walks. Open daily from 10 am to 5.30 pm in summer and 5 pm in winter (telephone: 0116 2710355).

WALKING ABOVE WATER: THE SADDINGTON TUNNEL

The Saddington Tunnel on the Grand Union Canal is 882 yards long and was completed in 1797. The walker cannot go through the tunnel but here you have the rare chance to walk above water! This interesting circuit also takes you along the feeder channel that links Saddington Reservoir with the canal and you finally return to the village over fields.

Saddington is an attractive red-brick village and the Queen's Head is a good starting point for this walk. From the garden of the pub there is an excellent view of the first part of the route and you can see the Saddington Reservoir, built to supply the canal. In the lovely valley nearby there is the canal feeder channel. One side of the valley rises steeply and there are spinneys and steep slopes all around in a lonely area. The walk reaches an aqueduct where the canal crosses the valley. The embankment here has been a problem. In 1865 it collapsed, nearly taking two boats and four people with it. In 1993 a serious leak required total reconstruction.

South of Kibworth Bridge on the Grand Union, a series of hills presented an obstacle to the canal engineers in the 18th century. They had no option but to tunnel. Hence, beginning with Saddington there are several tunnels on the canals to the south. Having walked on top of Saddington Tunnel, you turn from its north portal towards the village which you reach by crossing the fields south of Fleckney.

The Queen's Head is an Everard's house and can be relied on to provide excellent cask ales and good food. It has parking, a patio and garden, a restaurant and bar snacks and is most attractive both inside and out. Telephone: 0116 2402536. As an alternative you could try Jacqui's Tea Room at Barford House Farm, Mowsley Road, Saddington – about 1 mile out of the village. This is open on Friday, Saturday, Sunday and bank holidays from 11 am to 6 pm. There is a car park. Telephone: 0116 2402276.

- **HOW TO GET THERE:** From the M1 leave at junction 20 for the A4304 to Husbands Bosworth. Take the A5199, turning off at Mowsley for Saddington. From the A6 turn off at Kibworth Beauchamp for Smeeton Westerby and continue to Saddington.
- **PARKING:** At the Queen's Head (customers) with the permission of the landlord only. Otherwise there are a couple of places where a few cars can park on the village street, one being opposite the little Baptist chapel.
- **LENGTH OF THE WALK:** 3½ miles. Map OS Landranger 141 Kettering, Corby and surrounding area (GR 659919).

THE WALK

1. If you start at the Queen's Head car park you must walk away from the church along the main street, taking the Smeeton Westerby turn on the right so that you arrive at the Baptist chapel. Opposite this you see the sign 'Leicestershire Round Gumley 1¾ m'. Go down the narrow path, over a stile (marker post) and on ahead to another stile and marker post. Cross the field ahead to a metal gate at a stream. Go over a stile and the next stile to the right of a gate. Continue to another stile and footbridges. Turn left at the signpost to follow the stream on its left bank.

2. At the bridge carry on ahead. As the stream meanders right you bear left ahead to a stile (arrow) near trees. Go ahead along the woodland edge to a marker post at the far side of the field (another stream on your left). Carry on to the next marker post ahead in the trees. Continue ahead.

3. At the aqueduct go across the stile under the arch then turn left up onto the towpath. Go right along the towpath. As you come to the tunnel go up the path to walk over the top of the tunnel. Soon you arrive at the road between Saddington and Kibworth which you cross to continue your route. Shortly, you come to the north portal where the canal emerges from the tunnel. Turn left uphill here and follow the path alongside the hedge to a marker post, then over a stile to follow the path also alongside the hedge. At the corner of the field go over a gate and alongside the hedge to the main road. This is the Saddington to Fleckney road which can be very busy.

4. Cross the road to the gate on the opposite side. Go through and ahead alongside trees for about 200 yards. This is a bridlepath. At the end of the hedge on your right cross over to a marker post to the left. **Do not go straight on.** Now go ahead to the clump of trees in the dip in the middle of the field. This is a pond. There is a marker post here but it may be difficult to see.

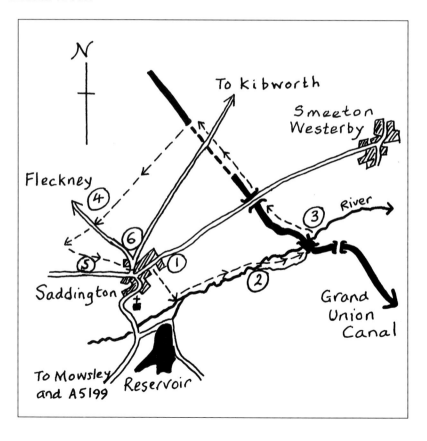

A stile leading to the towpath

5. Cross the ridge and furrow of this large field to the far side. There is a marker post to the left of two large trees. At the marker post cross stiles and go sharp left to a gate on the far left of the field. This leads onto the road.

6. Cross the road to follow the sign 'Leicestershire Round'. Go along a good pathway but in 100 yards turn right through a small gate in the trees (arrow). A narrow lane brings you to the village lane near the Baptist chapel where you started.

PLACES OF INTEREST NEARBY
Foxton Locks and Market Harborough are just a few miles to the south-east (see Walk 8). Further away, but well worth a visit, is *Stanford Hall* at Swinford, south of Lutterworth. Built in the 1690s, the Hall contains antique furniture, pictures and costumes. The grounds include a walled rose garden, a nature trail, a craft centre and a shop. There is a *Motorcycle Museum* with a replica of Percy Pilcher's 1898 flying machine. Open at weekends and bank holidays from Easter to the end of September 2.30 pm to 5.30 pm (telephone: 01788 860250). *Lutterworth Museum* in Churchgate is a small friendly museum with John Wycliffe associations. Open Monday, Thursday, Friday and Saturday, 10 am to 4 pm from mid February to mid November (telephone: 01455 284733).

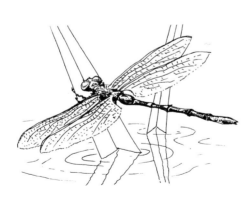

FOXTON LOCKS AND DEBDALE WHARF
♨♒♒

The canal revolution has left a wonderful legacy for walkers in Leicestershire. There are spectacular remains to be seen: beautiful brick bridges, aqueducts, cottages, inns, locks, inclined planes, reservoirs, canal feeders, tunnels, wharves, tramways and many old signs. Added to this are the lovely narrowboats which give so much colour and life to the waterways today. Foxton Locks is the embodiment of all these glorious things.

The view through Rainbow Bridge

The walk begins in the village of Foxton, situated ½ mile from the famous locks. There are many secret corners to explore: the old school, now a field centre, the nearby swingbridge which is turned to allow barges to pass through, the old court house near the tiny village green and, close by, the Baptist church of 1716.

Following the Market Harborough arm of the Grand Union Canal brings you to Foxton Locks at the Bottom Lock Basin end – a hive of activity. The whole scene is one of the most outstanding sights in Britain. There are ten locks which lift the canal 75 feet. Constructed between 1808 and 1814 they are a miracle of early 19th century engineering and completed the link between the Thames and the Humber. Recent and continuing restoration work has made the entire lock system a very fine sight, especially the inclined plane.

There is a shop at the Bottom Lock, also the Bridge 61 pub which has all the atmosphere inside redolent of the canal era. The conservatory and garden overlook the canal basin. There are snack meals, basket meals and main courses, with an all-day menu and a children's menu as well as a specials board. Much of the food is home-made and fresh bread is available. This is a freehouse and the classic Everards Old Original is there alongside Beacon and Tiger, also Adnams Bitter, Beamish Stout, Guinness on draught, Carlsberg lager and Stowford Press cider. Telephone: 0116 2792285.

The walk continues along the towpath to Debdale Wharf where there is a dry dock for narrowboats. At this point the walker turns south across the fields via a bridlepath to return to the village.

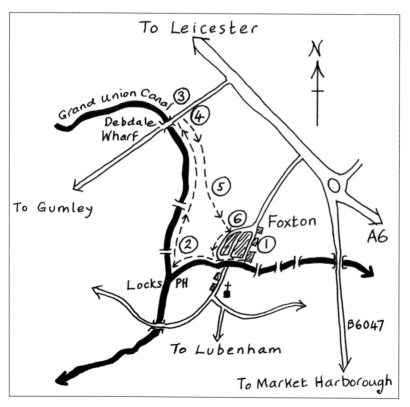

- **HOW TO GET THERE:** From Market Harborough take the A4304 and turn off at Lubenham or take the B6047 out of town to the north and you will see the left turn to Foxton in about 2 miles.
- **PARKING:** There is an excellent car park next to the village hall in Middle Street, Foxton. Next to it is a children's playground and recreation field with seats.
- **LENGTH OF THE WALK:** 3 miles. Map: OS Landranger 141 Kettering, Corby and surrounding area (GR 701899).

THE WALK

1. Start at the village hall car park in Middle Street. Turn left to Woodgate, with the field centre on your left. You have reached the canal. Turn right to follow the towpath to Foxton Bottom Lock and Basin about ½ mile away.

2. At the Basin keep right under Rainbow Bridge 62 and carry on along the towpath to Debdale Wharf, a distance of about 1¼ miles.

3. At Debdale Wharf Bridge 65 go under, turn right and ascend to the road. Now turn left down the road towards two houses. Do not bother about the bridlepath sign on your left but notice the footpath sign a little further on, also on the left. Here, turn right through a metal gate and over a stile (arrow).

4. Go about 80 yards and at the corner of trees on your right you will see a bridlepath sign. Cross the field as the sign indicates to the far corner. Here, a track through the hedge leads to a metal gate (arrow). You are next to and below the canal on your right. Go ahead alongside the hedge on your right, through a hand gate at the corner of the field into a narrow, wooded path which is near the canal.

5. Go through a hand gate and cross a large, arable field to an open gate at the far corner. You see Foxton ahead with the church on the hill.

6. When you arrive at the village, turn right into the lovely country lane. Follow it round to the main road and canal bridge. Continue into Middle Street to return to the car park near the village hall.

PLACES OF INTEREST NEARBY

See the *stairway of locks* and visit the *Canal Museum*, open Easter to October 10 am to 5 pm daily, October to Easter 11 am to 4 pm, closed Monday and Tuesday (telephone: 0116 2792657). Narrowboats can be hired by the day and there are cruises (telephone: 0116 2792285). *Market Harborough* is a rare example of a medieval 'new town'; St Dionysius' church has a superb spire and outstanding location near the 17th century timber-framed Old Grammar School; the Harborough Museum has displays of local history and there is a fine market on Tuesdays, Fridays and Saturdays.

Foxton Locks

ALONG THE GRAND UNION THROUGH THE LAUGHTON HILLS

The secret village of Laughton, near Market Harborough, lies high above the Grand Union Canal, a few miles from the famous Foxton Locks. This walk embraces field tracks, country lanes and one of the most lovely towpaths you could discover.

The ambitious scheme to link the Trent and London by waterway resulted in the Union Canal Bill, passed through Parliament in 1793. Its aim was to provide a canal from the Soar at Aylestone Bridge to the Grand Junction near Northampton. Once complete, this would be the last link in 'the great line of canals which extend from the Thames to the Humber'.

However, as a result of war, economies, local opposition, tunnels and increasing expense, the link was delayed. Work stopped at Debdale, just north of Foxton, in 1797 and did not resume until 1810. The stretch along the foot of the Laughton Hills, past Husbands Bosworth to the Grand Junction at Long Buckby in Northamptonshire was not opened until 1814.

Once a useful commercial artery, now the canal is an impressive recreational amenity which in the Laughton Hills is truly beautiful. As W.G. Hoskins writes: 'The canals of Leicestershire provide some of the most attractive rural scenery... and the best walking. They afford some scores of miles of quiet, carefree ambling, far from noise, diesel fumes, and the dangers of the open roads.'

Laughton is virtually a cul-de-sac, thankfully. It has a serenity and timeless quality. It even has a red telephone box and a seat close by. Opposite is a noble oak which frames the village buildings as you sit admiring the view. The walk begins here and a sense of joy and freedom overcomes you as you walk through the fields, lanes and towpath in this most English landscape.

So secluded is this walk that you will not find a pub en route. However, only $1\frac{1}{4}$ miles away is the Staff of Life at Mowsley. This very excellent family pub has a spacious lounge, an impressive conservatory restaurant, a terrace and a patio. There is a good car park at the rear. Marston's Pedigree Bitter, Church End Avon Ale and other real ales are available with draught Guinness, Foster's and Stella Artois lager and Strongbow cider. There is a food bar with a good choice of bar snacks and meals. A great deal is home-made, such as beef ale pie and spicy fish cake. There are many unusual main courses on the boards, for example halibut steak with lobster sauce, also at least nine speciality coffees. This freehouse has fresh fish daily, locally produced vegetables and a special Sunday Carvery from 12 noon to 5 pm. Lunches and evening dinners are available seven days a week. Telephone: 0116 2402359.

The Staff of Life, Mowsley

- **HOW TO GET THERE:** Leave the A5199 about 3 miles north of Husbands Bosworth, turning off eastwards to Mowsley and then following the sign to Laughton. If approaching from the A4304, turn off at Lubenham and follow signs to Laughton.
- **PARKING:** Sensible parking in the village streets is possible but please do not inconvenience residents in this most quiet of places.
- **LENGTH OF THE WALK:** 3½ miles. Map: OS Landranger 141 Kettering, Corby and surrounding area (GR 660890).

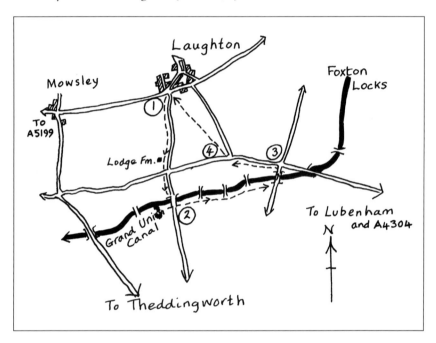

THE WALK

1. Go through the metal gate to the right of the telephone box and along the grass track, eventually passing Lodge Farm on your right. You arrive at the Lubenham-Mowsley road. Cross into a shady lane and continue downhill to the canal which you will see ahead. Go over the canal bridge and down the steps on the left, then through a gate and onto the towpath.

2. Turn right to follow the towpath to Bridge 56, a distance of about 1¼ miles. You will pass under other fine bridges on your way. At Bridge 56 turn right to go up to the lane. Then turn left to cross the bridge, going uphill to join the main road – known here as Bunkers Hill.

3. At the main road, turn left to follow it for about $\frac{3}{4}$ mile where, on the right, you see the lane leading to Laughton. There is a signpost, 'Laughton 1', to your left. Take care on the main road. It is not really busy but there will always be some traffic.

4. Do not go down the lane. Instead, at the footpath sign to the left of the lane cross the stile into the field. Now go to the marker on the far side, over a stile and across to the marker opposite. Follow marker posts over the remaining fields which are clearly visible and you return to your original track and the telephone box. One word of warning, when I walked this route in mid-summer, one field was high with rape, a path had not been cleared and this made walking difficult in this one place. If you prefer, you can return to Laughton via the lane instead of over the fields for $\frac{3}{4}$ mile.

PLACES OF INTEREST NEARBY

Foxton Locks on the well-used *Grand Union Canal* and *Foxton Canal Museum* (see Walk 9). *Foxton Boat Services Ltd* offers day boat hire (telephone: 0116 2792285). The medieval town of *Market Harborough* is a short distance to the east (see Walk 9).

THE RIVER SOAR AND ZOUCH LOCK

North of Loughborough, the River Soar meanders in a wide flood-plain. On one side is Leicestershire, on the other Nottinghamshire. East of Loughborough the Soar and the Grand Union Canal are well separated but a few miles downstream, at Zouch Lock, the canal reappears. Two interesting, attractive but very different villages face each other across the river – Hathern and Normanton on Soar. Walking along the riverbank is a wonderful delight.

Normanton on Soar

Hathern is a fairly large, compact village with its best parts off the busy A6. The area is a national communications hub with East Midlands Airport, the M1 and A42 only 4 miles away. Hathern lies in the triangle between Loughborough, Shepshed and Kegworth with Nottingham's city centre and Leicester's no more than 15 miles distant.

You can escape all this, however, by just taking a walk along the river from Hathern, across the fields to Zouch Lock and back, with only one brief traffic encounter. The Soar is acquiring a little more serenity and majesty hereabouts as it leaves urbanisation behind, soon to join the mighty Trent.

Although Hathern has many everyday buildings, if you look you will find the attractively situated St Peter and Paul's church, and not far away the old village cross and some cruck cottages. Buried in the churchyard is the Revd Andrew Glen (c1666–1732), one of Britain's earliest botanists and also vicar here from 1694–1732. He came as a young man and over the years collected many plants, some of which he sent to his friend John Ray, the distinguished botanist.

The Three Crowns is near the beginning and the end of your walk so you can choose when you will go. It is an Enterprise Freehouse and offers Bass on draught, Bass Cask Ale, Wadworth 6X, Highgate Ale and Caffrey's Irish, also Dry Blackthorn cider. You will find a skittle alley, a large beer garden, traditional pub games and good food. Telephone: 01509 842233.

Along the walk at Zouch Lock is the waterside Rose and Crown – in an ideal position to quench your thirst at the halfway point. There are bar snacks and restaurant meals, both at lunchtime and in the evenings, with many home-made dishes. Traditional ales are served and there is a fine view over the canal. Telephone: 01509 842240.

The marina at Zouch Lock

- **HOW TO GET THERE:**   Hathern is just north of Loughborough along the A6. Turn off down Wide Lane into the village.
- **PARKING:**   There are quiet spots near the church and in some other streets but be careful not to hinder the villagers.

• **LENGTH OF THE WALK:** 3½ miles. Map: OS Landranger 129 Nottingham and Loughborough area (GR 503224); also *Parish Walks and Rides in Leicestershire: Hathern* (Leicestershire County Council).

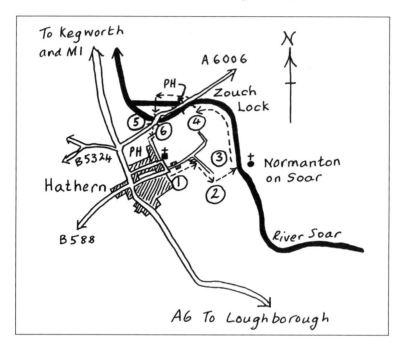

THE WALK

1. Start at the village cross in Hathern. The C of E primary school is on your right. Walk east past the post office and shop on your left. Go ahead to the school sign at the bend in the road. Walk on into the lane marked by a cul-de-sac sign. Carry on ahead with the primary school on your right. Ignore footpath signs to your left and right and carry on ahead. At a smallholding, turn right (marker post) along a wide path which soon narrows between bushes.

2. At a marker post on your right turn left towards a church spire (Normanton on Soar), along a rough field path. Ignore a marker post on the left and go on for 50 yards, bearing right at the next marker post. Soon, turn sharp left at the next marker, then immediately left along the field edge to the next marker about 50 yards away. Follow the path bearing right alongside the field towards houses. You arrive at the River Soar, opposite Normanton.

3. Turn left to walk beside the river along a grassy path to a marker post and stile about 100 yards away. Follow the riverside to the marina ahead and through a gate, continuing along the river (Soar Boating Club opposite). Pass through the next gate (marker post) and then another gate. At the sign 'Danger Weir', go through the gate to the left of the notice. If you wish to return to the village here, turn left at the stile and cross the field back to your original path.

4. To complete the full walk, turn right to cross the bridges over Zouch Weir. The Zouch Radial Gate was opened on 25th October 1995. Cross the busy main road carefully. Turn right over the road bridge, then left into a riverside/canal path. If you wish you can visit the Rose and Crown at this point. On your return to the canalside path continue for about 400 yards until you reach a footbridge over the canal. Cross this through a gate then over a field to another gate and marker post on the far side.

5. At the busy main road turn right along the footpath. Then over Zouch bridge back into Leicestershire. At a sign cross the road to the other footpath, over stiles (marker) for the path back to Hathern. Once over the stile bear left along the river via the next stile to a marker post. Then cross the field on your right diagonally to a yellow marker post.

6. Nearby is a kissing gate at the corner of the field. Go through to a marker post 25 yards on. This takes you to a field lane back to the village which is visible ahead. You turn left into another lane which soon brings you to the church and the Three Crowns.

PLACES OF INTEREST NEARBY
Charnwood Forest, from Hathern along the B588 and then south of Loughborough, offers viewpoints like Beacon Hill and Old John in Bradgate Park with excellent highland scenery. *John Taylor Bellfoundry Museum*, Freehold Street, Loughborough (telephone: 01509 233414). *Kegworth Museum*, 52 High Street (telephone: 01509 672886). *Donington Grand Prix Collection*, Castle Donington – the world's largest collection of Grand Prix racing cars (telephone: 01332 811027). *Whatton House Gardens* in Long Whatton: home-grown produce for sale, teas. Open from Easter to the end of August, every Sunday and Bank Holiday Monday, 2 pm to 6 pm (telephone: 01509 842268).

BARROW UPON SOAR AND QUORN: BY RIVER AND CANAL

The River Soar makes a large meander between Quorn and Barrow and the neck of the meander has been cut by a canal which is part of the Grand Union. There are lovely river and canalside views both from the Quorn and the Barrow areas. This walk follows the canal and then returns to Barrow along the Soar meander. Although traffic abounds in the region, this circuit is sedate, very rural and full of charm.

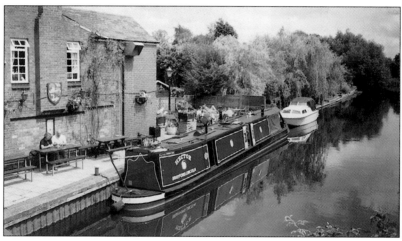

Boats moored alongside the Navigation Inn

Each settlement stands well above the floodplain, Barrow on the flanks of the Wolds and Quorn on the edge of Charnwood Forest. Railways and roads kept above the valley but now the new A6 goes through the middle, raised up on its embankments. Our walk goes over, then under, the A6.

This stroll has a delightful start. Mill Lane in Barrow leads to the canal, with a picturesque lock and bridge and the Navigation Inn nearby. Together they form an outstanding scene. The inn was built shortly after the opening of the canal in 1794 and still retains the old atmosphere, inside and out. On fine days you can sit on the patio, which gives you a good view of the ever-active canal traffic. The spacious interior has a definite 'canal feel' with low beams. There is plenty of choice for drinks with Shipstone's Bitter, Pedigree, Tetley, Banks and Taylor, Harrowby and Ermine Ale, Ansells Mild and Worthington, supported by Carling and Stella Artois lager, Strongbow cider and Guinness on draught. Food is available and includes excellent bar snacks (telephone: 01509 412842).

The walk proceeds along a delightful towpath with splendid views of the rear of properties and their waterfront, eventually reaching Barrow Deep Lock and the busy bridge carrying the B675 to Quorn. Here 'your cup runneth over' for you will find the Soar Bridge Inn and opposite the Riverside Inn. The former has family facilities, a patio, food, cask ales, skittles and petanque (telephone: 01509 412686). The latter has real ales, food, boating and a beer garden (telephone: 01509 412260).

You then go along 'the slabs', as the locals call the path to Quorn, and this is most pleasant and easy. Once in the leafy outskirts you will see many impressive buildings. Quorn has been the centre of the Quorn Hunt for many years. Tom Fir, 'one of the greatest huntsmen of all time', is buried in St Bartholomew's churchyard. Quorn Hall is close to the walk. If you need refreshment hereabouts call into the Bull's Head in Quorn's High Street for bar meals and restaurant service both at lunchtime and in the evenings (telephone 01509 412562).

Leaving Quorn the walk turns into a rural route again as you cross the valley over fields and return to the Navigation Inn.

- **HOW TO GET THERE:**   Barrow is near the A6. Once in the town look for Mill Lane – a little distance south of the main roundabout in the town. Go down Mill Lane to the end.
- **PARKING:**   As you approach the Navigation Inn you will need to park sensibly at some point in Mill Lane or along the road off it.
- **LENGTH OF THE WALK:**   3 miles. Map: OS Landranger 129 Nottingham and Loughborough area (GR 577168).

THE WALK

1. Start at the Navigation Inn. Go over the canal bridge (No 28) and turn right to follow the towpath. Shortly, you arrive at Barrow Deep Lock. Go over the bridge and ahead to the main road. At present, work is taking place to make a small garden here with a pathway through to Barrow Bridge – thus cutting the corner.

2. The Soar Bridge Inn and the Riverside Inn are now very close. Turn left over the bridge which is usually very busy with traffic. Immediately, go through a rustic kissing gate to your left and along the path ahead known as 'the slabs'.

3. Soon you cross the A6 via a long footbridge then go through a gate into a tree-lined avenue. Quorn Hall is on your left. Turn left into the main road and follow this round as it bears right (Soar Road). You are alongside the river and you get glimpses of it, but mostly there are houses or gardens in the way.

4. You cross a small stream and there is a park to your right. At the T junction turn left, signposted Mountsorrel. Go past the impressive village hall, built in local granite, and also the Quorn Country Hotel. Pass the signpost for Swithland and keep ahead for about 200 yards until opposite No. 59 you see a footpath sign on your left. Go through a kissing gate into the field path.

5. Go across the field to a footbridge in the hedge opposite then follow the riverbank ahead towards the pylon. The grass track eventually moves slightly away from the river, through a hedge, and ahead to the next gap in the hedge (a dome and chimney mark the way in front). Go across a stile and ahead to a marker arrow on the far side. Cross the footbridge. You are now at the riverside again.

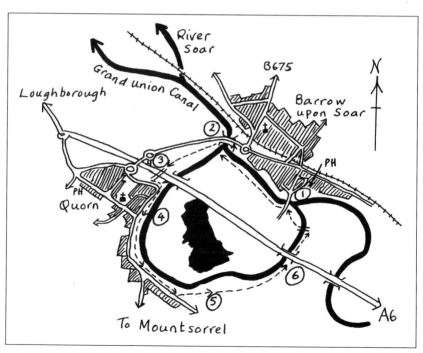

6. Carry on alongside the river, under the A6 and ahead to a marker post in the hedge, still following the river. Over a stile, bear left to cross a footbridge and follow the 'slabs' to the right. Go over the stile, turn right into a lane which soon leads you back to the Navigation Inn.

PLACES OF INTEREST NEARBY

There is plenty to see and do in this area. *Whatoff Lodge Farm* west of Quorn is a 200-acre working farm with a museum and shop, also facilities for picnics (telephone: 01509 412127). *Great Central Railway* – Britain's only main line steam railway – runs between Loughborough and Leicester via Rothley and Quorn. Weekday trains are scheduled from June to September inclusive, also every weekend and on bank holidays throughout the year. You can drive a locomotive and have a super meal on board, if you wish (telephone: 01509 230726). *Loughborough Market* is one of the finest street markets in the country. Held in the Market Place and town centre every Thursday and Saturday (telephone: 01509 218113). *The Carillon and War Memorial*, Queen's Park, Loughborough has a museum of the armed forces and bell recitals. Views from the tower are magnificent. Open seven days a week (telephone: 01509 634704). All the wonderful attractions of *Charnwood Forest* – Beacon Hill, Bradgate Park and so on – are only a few miles to the west.

The lock at Barrow on Soar

COSSINGTON MILL: WHERE THE WREAKE MEETS THE SOAR

The River Wreake joins the River Soar about 6 miles north of Leicester. Here there is a profusion of water - lakes, rivers and canals - on the very wide floodplain. The lovely village of Cossington stands above it, occupying a wedge of land between the Soar and Wreake. This walk begins near the church and then continues across the floodplain, following the Soar riverbank to Cossington Mill. It returns to the village via a series of lakes produced by gravel excavation in the past, now an attractive part of the scenery.

The race at Cossington Lock

Cossington is an attractive linear village, neat, tidy and prosperous. There are a number of old cruck cottages and historic buildings. Near the war memorial, with All Saints' church behind and Magpie Cottage to the right, is a cameo scene of what an English village should look like. In the churchyard is the grave of Lord Kitchener's father who died in 1894. He lived in the old Manor House. South of the church is the old rectory which dates back, in part, to the 16th century. Pevsner describes this as 'one of the best small buildings in the county'. You will have a good view of this house as you end your walk.

As you cross the floodplain towards the River Soar you see Charnwood Forest in front and, behind, the silhouette of Cossington and Sileby. Along the riverbank all is quiet, even though the A6 traffic thunders nearby. Eventually you reach Cossington Lock and close by Osier Cottage, dated 1875. Soon you see Cossington Mill, certainly dating from the 13th century and possibly from Domesday times.

Take the time to make a short diversion down to look at Cossington Mill, now a restaurant. The fare here includes two-course lunches served from Tuesday to Saturday (telephone: 01509 812205). From Cossington Lock there is a lovely walk along the bank of the Wreake. Soon you turn off between lakes to return to Cossington village via a large gravel working. To quench your thirst you could visit the Royal Oak, located in the main street. You will find a good range of Everards beers, a garden/patio, food and skittles as well as a congenial atmosphere. Telephone: 01509 813937.

- **HOW TO GET THERE:** From the A6 turn off on the B5328 to reach Cossington. From the A46 join the same B road via the A607.
- **PARKING:** Though some parking is possible in the village street this is usually too busy and the best place is to park near the church which is reached via a short lane off the main street.
- **LENGTH OF THE WALK:** 3 miles: Map: OS Landranger 129 Nottingham and Loughborough area (GR 604138).

The delightful village of Cossington

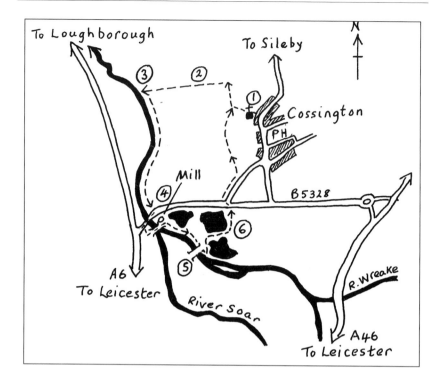

THE WALK

1. Start in the churchyard. Cross to the gate opposite (yellow post). Turn left along a path to the next post, about 100 yards ahead. Go over the stile then turn right. This is a pleasant walk in grassland. Now go left over a stile and plank bridge with trees on your right. In about 100 yards turn left at right angles alongside a hedge. There is a yellow post to show this but it may be hidden in the undergrowth.

2. As the hedge ends look for a marker post ahead. Go over the stile and cross a rough road (Heavy Plant Crossing), into a wide track ahead (post). Keep going over the next rough road with trees on your right. At the river, turn left along a grassy path.

3. Follow the river and the path as it bends around a wood which is on your right. Markers show that the actual path is **through** the wood but since this is very overgrown walkers have chosen to go around. At a plank bridge and stile go ahead to the riverbank. Cross a stile to the left of a wooden gate. Carry on bearing left along the riverbank past a dead tree. Bear left round a paddock to a marker post on the left of the poplars. In about 30 yards you reach a stile in trees and a plank bridge (Angling Club nearby). Go up steps to the busy road, the B5328.

4. To see Cossington Mill cross over the road and go down the short lane. Return the same way to the main road, then turn left over Cossington Bridge. At the marker post go left down to the lock. Then go over the footbridge and stile to continue along the riverbank.

5. At a large metal bridge follow two marker posts to go underneath. Carry on along the riverside to a metal stile. Turn left as marker post indicates. Go over the field diagonally between lakes to a wooden gate and path at the far hedge.

6. Turn left alongside the lake to reach the main road. Cross the road carefully into Platt's Lane where there is a footpath. Look for a sign and stile on your left. Go over and follow a path round the side of a quarry. In 100 yards go over another stile then turn right, aiming for a marker post. You are walking towards the church which you will soon reach via gates and plank bridges, mostly bearing right to meet the path where you started.

PLACES OF INTEREST NEARBY

Stonehurst Family Farm and Motor Museum in Bond Lane, Mountsorrel, has farm animals, rabbits, guinea pigs, a cuddle corner, free tractor rides, a farm walk, a collection of vintage cars and motor cycles, a working blacksmith's forge and a farm shop (telephone: 01509 413216). *Sileby Boat Yard* in Mill Lane, Sileby hires out small narrowboats for day trips. Open from April to the end of October, 9 am to 6 pm (telephone: 01509 813583). All the attractions of *Charnwood Forest* are only a few miles to the west.

KING LEAR'S LAKE AT WATERMEAD COUNTRY PARK

The River Soar flows through the heart of the city of Leicester and joins the River Trent some 20 miles further north. Its wide floodplain has been excavated for sand and gravel for many years and this is still happening. At Watermead Country Park in Birstall old gravel workings are now lakes. This is only 4 miles away from the city centre yet it is a haven for wildlife and a delight for walkers with over 200 acres of nature reserve and woodlands and designated picnic areas.

King Lear's Lake

This walk starts near Birstall Lock on a canalised part of the River Soar. Above the lock is the old village. Following the waterway soon brings you to Watermead Country Park where the river and canal diverge. There are few landmarks to show the way in this low-lying area – it is reminiscent of the Fens in the time of Hereward the Wake, when the Normans searched in vain to find his hideout.

Often you are walking on a causeway with water each side, sometimes in open grassland, sometimes in woodland. Everywhere there are ducks, geese, magpies, swans, a heron or two and other birds. Eventually you reach the largest lake – King Lear's Lake – so called because, as legend tells, in the eighth century BC Britain was ruled by King Lear. On his death he was buried in a chamber beneath the River Soar, downstream from Leicester (the town named after him). Could this have been the place? A fine sculpture shows Shakespeare's final scene where Lear kneels to mourn his daughter Cordelia. The Earl of Kent and the Duke of Albany look on in pity. This delightful circuit has many seats and picnic tables en route, so if you wish you could take your refreshments with you. Alternatively, you could visit the White Horse, a Big Steak pub, situated just near Birstall Lock in White Horse Lane. It has a lovely beer garden and children's play area. Inside there is a comfortable, attractively furnished L-shaped lounge. An excellent choice of beers is on offer with Tetley, Pedigree and Ansells Bitter, also Foster's, Carlsberg and Stella Artois lager and draught Guinness. Blackthorn cider is available too. A wide choice of food includes lighter snacks, pasta dishes, salads, hot platters, fish platters, steaks and desserts. Children are welcome up to 9 pm and dogs on leads are allowed in the garden. Open all day for food and drink, weekdays 11.30 am to 11 pm (food 12 noon to 10 pm), Sundays 12 noon to 10.30 pm. Telephone: 0116 2674490.

The fine sculpture on King Lear's Lake

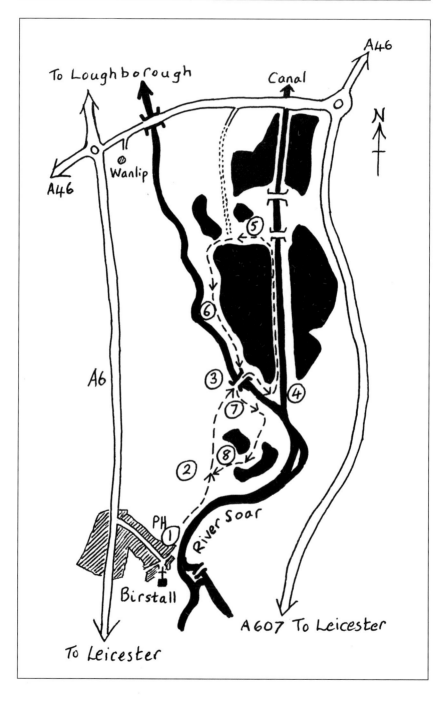

- **HOW TO GET THERE:** Leave the A6 Leicester-Loughborough road following signs to Birstall village centre. At the roundabout in the village look for blue notices indicating the 'Leicester via Watermead' cycle route. This leads you down Whiles Lane to Birstall Lock.
- **PARKING:** There is quiet roadside parking opposite houses and next to the river in Whiles Lane. Alternatively, with the permission of the landlord and if you are a customer, in the car park of the White Horse.
- **LENGTH OF THE WALK:** $2\frac{1}{2}$ miles. Map: OS Landranger 140 Leicester and Coventry area and 129 Nottingham and Loughborough area are both needed (GR 599090).

THE WALK

1. Walk north along the riverside path with houses on your left. Go through a gate with a yellow marker post. A sign welcomes you to Watermead Country Park.

2. Carry on the tarmac path, following the sign 'Meadow Lane Car Park $\frac{1}{4}$ m'. You reach a fourways signpost. Go forward, following the sign to 'King Lear's Lake $\frac{3}{4}$ m' and walking next to a lake on your right. In the distance ahead you will see a large bridge.

3. Go over the bridge and in front of you is King Lear's Lake. Turn right to follow a well-marked path round the lake.

4. On reaching a metal gate and bridge turn left to continue round the lake. As you walk you will have King Lear's Lake on your left and the Grand Union Canal on your right.

5. Bear left around the lake. Here you will see signs advertising 'Day Fishing'. Warnings about blue/green algae advise keeping dogs out of the water and, of course, swimming is prohibited.

6. Complete the circuit of the lake, looking at the sculpture of King Lear, then go back across the bridge which you crossed earlier, to your right.

7. Turn left immediately, once over the bridge, to follow a grass path, signposted 'Thurmaston $\frac{3}{4}$ m'. Keep to the main grass path. At a metal gate on your left go into a woodland path. In 100 yards this opens out to a lakeside and picnic area.

8. Follow the lakeside path into the trees between two water areas, over a wooden bridge. Turn left at a T junction of paths. You are now on your original path. At the signpost go straight on down 'Whiles Lane to Birstall ½ m', keeping to the tarmac path. Carry on to your start, continuing to Birstall Lock and the White Horse.

PLACES OF INTEREST NEARBY
Leicester city centre is only 4 miles to the south and you can continue your riverside walk into the city if you wish. Only a mile away on this route is *Belgrave Hall* and gardens, a delightful three-storey Queen Anne house dating from 1709 with its own ghost (telephone: 0116 2666590). Nearby is *Abbey Pumping Station* with its public health displays, unique Victorian beam engines and an interactive toilet (telephone: 0116 2661330). *Bradgate Park*, 850 acres of medieval deer park, once the home of Lady Jane Grey, Nine Days Queen of England, is only 5 miles to the west. Here there is the ruin of Bradgate House and a visitor centre (telephone: 0116 2362713) with a shop. Rocky hills, woods, heath, bracken, parkland with red and fallow deer make this an excellent place for a family picnic.

WALK 14

RAMBLING ALONG THE WREAKE

Asfordby, Frisby on the Wreake and Kirby Bellars are villages situated above the floodplain of the River Wreake as it flows from Melton Mowbray to join the River Soar at Cossington. Between the villages there is a lakeside created by former gravel workings. Wonderful secret walks will take you right into the waterways which will be on both sides of your path and there are glorious distant views of church spires with swans gliding in the foreground.

Looking across the water towards Asfordby

It is a delight to get off the busy A607 at Kirby Bellars and, within a few minutes, find yourself at an apparent 'dead-end' with the oddly eroded marlstone tower of St Peter's shining in the sun. Once there was a priory nearby and the pastoral presence of the floodplain of the River Wreake. To the car this is a cul-de-sac but, thankfully, to the walker it is just the beginning of a walk on the wild side.

For a series of paths infiltrate the wetlands hereabouts, so close sometimes that you feel you are walking on water. You progress towards the spire of Asfordby's All Saints' church, though never reach it, since you follow the Wreake and then rise up into Frisby. Arthur Mee wrote, some sixty years ago, that 'Nature and Art have both been kind to this village on the Wreake (Asfordby)... a charming picture of rural serenity' - now the distant view still supports this claim but nearer acquaintance shows the mark of modern times. The nearness to Leicester, Melton and even Nottingham has given new life to the villages along the Wreake since they are all so convenient for commuters.

Although you are not always conscious of it down on the floodplain, both busy road and railway are close by. Once the Wreake was navigable and so, in past times, the valley was a communications artery. Frisby is surprisingly large with many historic houses and there are numerous lovely gardens and quiet corners to observe. The church has the unusual dedication in these parts to St Thomas of Canterbury.

The Bell Inn at Frisby has low beams and a long lounge with plenty of room. There is a good car park, and off it a children's room. Tetley Bitter, Abbot Ale and Marston's are among the ales served, alongside Guinness on draught, Blackthorn cider, Castlemaine XXXX and Stella Artois lager. A full menu is available on weekdays from 12 noon to 1.30 pm and 6 pm to 8.30 pm; Sundays 12 noon to 1.30 pm and 7 pm to 8.30 pm. Telephone: 01664 434237.

- **HOW TO GET THERE:** Use the A607 between Leicester and Melton Mowbray to reach Kirby Bellars, which is only about 3 miles from the latter.
- **PARKING:** Near the church at Kirby Bellars which is quiet and out of the way.
- **LENGTH OF THE WALK:** $3\frac{1}{2}$ miles. Map: OS Landranger 129 Nottingham and Loughborough area (GR 718183).

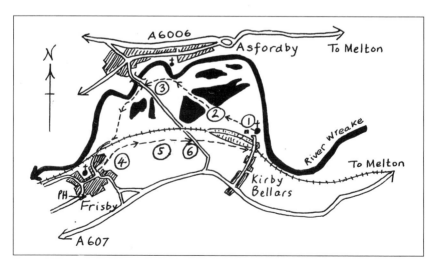

The Bell Inn, Frisby

THE WALK

1. Start at the church. Go through an open gate and bear left (there is a stile next to the gate). You come to a nursery. Turn right here and continue between trees. At a locked wooden gate climb the stile and turn left as the arrow shows. Go diagonally across the field to a clump of trees (marker) with lakes close by.

2. Climb the stile (arrow) near to a lifebelt. Walk now between two lakes. The spire of Asfordby church is ahead. At a stile, cross and go diagonally to the next marker post near the river. Follow the riverbank as marker posts show the way. You come to another stile near a row of trees, then a metal gate, a gap and a wooden kissing gate. On your left is a busy road. Follow alongside the hedge and river on your right. At a stile in the corner of the field bear right alongside the river. At a marker post you emerge from the path onto the road.

3. Turn right and cross the road carefully to a footpath sign at the side of the bridge. Go over the stile to follow the path, bearing right. Now go ahead to a marker post; **do not** go to your right. At a stile Frisby church spire shows the route ahead. Cross the field and keep following marker posts, bridges and stiles until you reach a narrow field next to the railway line. At the end of the field cross the railway line into a rough village lane which eventually becomes Mill Lane.

4. On reaching the top of the hill at Church View Barn (on your right), turn left at the footpath sign for the walk back to Kirby Bellars across the fields. Before doing so you should have a break to look round Frisby and to visit the Bell Inn. On resuming your walk, go up the house drive to a five-bar gate. Then cross the field to the left, making for a marker post and stile. Follow arrows across the field to another marker post to the left of a pylon. Then over a double stile and plank bridge ahead towards the spire of Kirby Bellars church.

5. At the corner of the field take the stile on your right (**not left**). Cross the double stile/bridge and go ahead alongside the hedge on your left. Carry on ahead through the field as the marker post indicates. Keep ahead at a path crossroads. There may be a great deal of undergrowth/crop to walk through here.

6. You reach a busy road. Cross to the stile opposite and continue to the far left corner of the field, with houses in view. Go over a double stile, across a field and through a kissing gate into the village lane at Kirby Bellars. Marker posts will have shown the way. Turn left to return to your car at the church.

PLACES OF INTEREST NEARBY

Melton Mowbray with its Tuesday cattle market and general street market, its famous pork pies and its Stilton cheese is only 3 miles away. *Hollies Farm* at Little Dalby is a few miles to the south of Melton. This is a fine furniture workshop and showroom with a tearoom serving home-made cakes/biscuits. Open Monday to Saturday, 9 am to 5 pm; tearoom Easter to October, Saturday, Sunday and Bank Holiday Mondays, 10.30 am to 4.30 pm (telephone: 01664 454553).

GRANTHAM CANAL AND THE VALE OF BELVOIR

The *200-year-old Grantham Canal links a series of quiet villages, providing a very pleasant towpath walk between each. All lie on fertile, level ground in the lovely Vale of Belvoir. Above to the east, is the escarpment on which Belvoir Castle is situated.*

A bridge over the Grantham Canal

The Grantham Canal was opened in 1797 and though traffic declined with the advent of the railways it did not officially close until 1936. There are 18 locks between Nottingham and Grantham as the canal falls 139 feet, but none in our section. Coal, roadstone, lime and nightsoil once came into the area and farming produce went out.

This walk begins near the village of Plungar and, in fact, the latter part of the route passes through the village. The church has a rare dedication to St Helen, patron saint of dyers, nailsmiths, needlemakers and wells. Can you find Reynard the Fox carved on a stone plaque on the outside west wall of the tower?

The Anchor Inn is in the middle of Plungar and reflects the nearness to the 'navigation'. It is an unpretentious building with food at lunchtime and in the evenings, Mansfield and guest ales and a beer garden. Telephone: 01949 860589.

- **HOW TO GET THERE:**   Plungar is situated in the area between the A606 Melton Mowbray–Nottingham road, the A52 Grantham–Nottingham road and the A46/A607 Melton–Grantham road. Whichever major road you approach by, look for signs to Belvoir Castle as this will help you to find this rather obscure village.

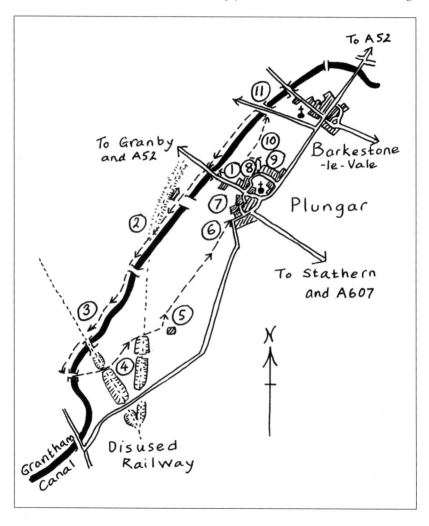

- **PARKING:** The best place is in a rough layby near the canal start, opposite Grange Farm on Granby Road. This road is easy to find as it leads out of the village from the Anchor Inn. Otherwise, if you prefer to leave your car in the village itself, there are many quiet places for sensible parking.
- **LENGTH OF THE WALK:** $2\frac{1}{2}$ miles or 4 miles, the full walk taking you north of Plungar and including a further stretch along the canal. Map: OS Landranger 129 Nottingham and Loughborough (GR 767343) also *Parish Walks and Rides in Leicestershire: Redmile Barkestone-le-Vale and Plungar* (Leicestershire County Council).

The Walk

1. Start where Granby Road crosses the canal. This is near Grange Farm and a building which was once J. Pell & Son, Butcher, as a sign indicates. Turn left to go down onto the towpath through a gap next to a metal gate.

2. Carry on along the towpath for about a mile. You will pass a farm, cross a disused railway line and see Bridge 47. The canal almost disappears beneath vegetation.

3. At Bridge 46A go under and carry on bearing left along the towpath. Soon you come to a concrete bridge on your left. Cross over (arrow) and go ahead uphill on a rough path.

4. At a yellow marker post cross a bridge over another disused railway line. This may be overgrown. The next marker indicates right alongside a hedge with the village of Plungar now in view.

5. At the corner of the field (marker post) go over the stile then diagonally left to the next marker post. Climb over stiles to cross the field again diagonally left to a marker post in the far corner near the houses.

6. On reaching the corner of the field follow marker posts over stiles to the left, avoiding the houses. Follow the wooden fence through a gate to the left of the pylon, alongside a hedge. At the corner of the field cross a stile into a village lane.

7. Go left down Frog Lane then continue left down The Gas which becomes a narrow path leading to Post Office Lane. The Old Post Office is on your right. Note the VR post box. At this point, if you wish, you can turn left at the Anchor Inn and return to your start.

A narrow stretch of the Grantham Canal

8. If you wish to complete the full walk, carry on into Church Lane opposite. Follow this round until you come to a footpath sign on your left, just before Delta 4 cottage. Go through the hedge and you find yourself in a lovely garden. Go right to find a post which takes you into a paddock.

9. Go diagonally left across this rough area to the far corner. Follow the arrow here through undergrowth alongside the hedge. Halfway along, a marker post indicates that you must go right over a stile into a field.

10. Go ahead towards the spire of Barkestone church. You will cross four fields and all you need to do is to look for the marker posts. There may be rough parts in the final field. On reaching the fourth field make for the far left corner which has a marker post. Here you will find you are very close to Bridge 50 on the canal.

11. Cross the bridge to join the towpath on your left. Follow this for about $\frac{3}{4}$ mile to return to your starting point on Granby Road.

PLACES OF INTEREST NEARBY

Belvoir Castle is the outstanding attraction nearby. This is the home of the Duke and Duchess of Rutland with magnificent staterooms, notable pictures, tapestries and fine furniture. The Queen's Royal Lancers Museum is here also. There are many special events held at the Castle. Open from the end of March to the end of September; Sundays only in October (telephone: 01476 870262). *Uncle Nork's Tearoom and Farm*, Langar Lane, Harby has a toddlers' play area as well as pigs, goats, sheep, ducks, geese, ponies and rabbits. Open daily in summer (not Tuesday and Wednesday), 11 am to 5 pm; Saturdays and Sundays only in winter, 11.30 to 4 pm (telephone: 01949 861146). *Tumbledown Farm* in Spinney Road, Melton Mowbray is a traditional working farm open all year except 24/26 December (telephone: 01664 481811).

RUTLAND WATER: BARNSDALE

Barnsdale is one of four major picnic sites around Rutland Water, England's largest lowland reservoir (see Walk 17). It is located on the north shore only 3 miles from the county town, Oakham. Its terraced arrangement makes it one of the most distinctive and attractive of all the sites. Walks through woodland and near the shoreline, as this one, are allied to splendid views across the water.

A view of Rutland Water from Barnsdale

Once there was a village of Barnsdale which has now vanished. Today the Viking Way and the Hereward Way meet here. Barnsdale Hall Hotel and Country Club has been developed on the flanks of the hill around the former hunting lodge of the Earl Fitzwilliam. The main Hall and stables still stand as they were in 1892 and are now holiday ownership apartments and hotel rooms. Nearby there are holiday chalets, the whole complex occupying 65 acres overlooking Rutland Water. The public can use the bars and restaurant (telephone: 01572 757901) and there is a full range of food which includes snacks such as home-made soup and club sandwiches.

At Barnsdale Picnic Park itself you will find the Drought Garden and Arboretum designed by the late Geoff Hamilton. This is open daily and entry is free. There are mature specimens of the main tree varieties planted around Rutland Water during its construction in the 1970s. Geoff Hamilton began his BBC gardening series at a small cottage which you will pass on the walk but due to the success of the programme he moved to larger premises on Exton Avenue nearby.

The walk takes you along the shoreline below Barnsdale Hall and Country Club, then up the hill overlooking the area, giving one of Rutland's most outstanding views. About here you pass Barnsdale Lodge Hotel which is a good place to stop for a drink and a snack or a more substantial meal if you wish. Here, the Edwardian dining rooms and conservatory restaurant with à la carte and buttery menus offer a good choice, supported by a range of traditional ales. Morning coffee and afternoon teas are also served. Outside you will find a herb garden, patio and children's play area. There are good views over Rutland Water and Geoff Hamilton's Barnsdale Gardens are just down the road. Telephone: 01572 724678.

Holiday chalets in the grounds of Barnsdale Country Club

- **HOW TO GET THERE:**   From Stamford and the A1 follow the A606 towards Empingham and Oakham. From the A47 at Uppingham follow the A6003 to Oakham, then the A606.

- **PARKING:** There is ready-made parking at the Anglian Water Barnsdale Picnic Park but a charge is made (pay & display). You can use your ticket at any other Rutland Water Picnic Parks on the same day.
- **LENGTH OF THE WALK:** 2 miles. Map: OS Explorer 15 Rutland Water and Stamford (GR 909087).

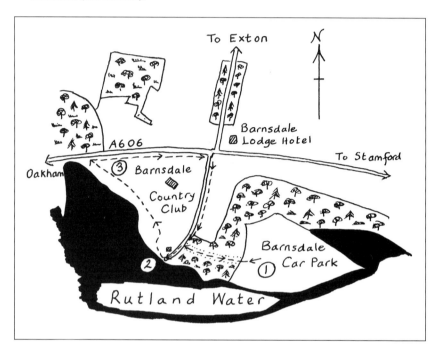

THE WALK

1. Start in the Barnsdale Car Park. Retrace your steps through the woods back to the approach road. At the T junction turn left downhill with good views of the reservoir.

2. When you reach the gates across the road go through and in 30 yards turn right into the field path. Follow this round for about ½ mile until you arrive at the A606.

3. Do not go onto the road but turn sharp right as you emerge from the gate to follow a path which does lead to the road higher up the hill. Carry on along the footpath. At the top of the hill look back to see a great view. Now, if you wish, you can cross the road to go to Barnsdale Lodge Hotel. Otherwise, just turn right downhill and in a short distance you will come to the lane on your left which takes you back through the woods to your starting point.

PLACES OF INTEREST NEARBY

There are many interesting places very close to Barnsdale. *Geoff Hamilton's famous BBC gardens* are on The Avenue, Exton, a little way from Barnsdale Lodge Hotel. Open daily from March to November, 10 am to 5 pm (telephone: 01572 813200). *Exton village* is only a mile further on and here you have a classic English village with a green, thatched cottages, a pub and, some distance off, the church of SS Peter and Paul, with its nationally famous sculptures. *Greetham Garden Centre and Falconry* is 3 miles to the north. There is a tearoom. Open daily 9 am to 5 pm; Sundays 10 am to 5 pm (telephone: 01572 813100). *Rutland Railway Museum*, Ashwell Road, Cottesmore is open at weekends, 11 am to 5 pm, with steam days regularly as advertised (telephone: 01572 813203). *Oakham*, the nearest town, has interesting shops and many other attractions, including *Oakham Castle* (telephone: 01572 723654). For more details contact the Tourist Information Centre (telephone: 01572 724329). Of course Rutland Water with all its amenities is to hand with the *Anglian Water Bird Watching Centre* at Egleton (telephone: 01572 770651) and *Lyndon Hill Visitor Centre and Nature Reserve* (telephone: 01572 737378) .

RUTLAND WATER: NORMANTON

Rutland Water is England's largest lowland reservoir. Built in the 1970s to supply water to potentially expanding towns like Peterborough, it now also has a major role as a leisure focus. Four picnic parks, each distinctive (see Walk 16), facilities such as cycling, sailing and fishing, and a pleasure boat for cruises, all combine to draw visitors to the area. It is a paradise for walkers especially, with a perimeter of 26 miles and many paths to discover in safety. This outstanding circuit is based on Normanton Picnic Park.

The jetty on Rutland Water

Normanton is on the south shore of Rutland Water, near the village of Edith Weston and the Sailing Centre. The dam is just a mile to the north-east. A landmark is Normanton Tower, once the church of St Matthew, now a water museum. Nearby is Normanton Park Hotel which was once the stable block of a great mansion of the Earl of Ancaster. In the 18th century the mansion, the church and the village of Normanton stood close together. However, in the desire to empark the area, the owner moved the villagers to his model village of Empingham nearby in 1764.

So, even before the reservoir arrived, the landscape changed. A village disappeared. Then due to heavy commitments, the Earl of Ancaster of the day had to part with the house in 1925. It could not be sold intact and it was demolished and the estate split up. Rutland Water, some 50 years later, completed the landscape changes.

In place of an aristocratic preserve we now have a most public playground, open all year dawn to dusk. The Bird Watching Centre at Egleton and the Nature Reserve are outstanding attractions and there is a Butterfly Farm and Aquatic Centre at Syke's Lane, Empingham. For further information contact Rutland Water Tourist Information Centre (telephone: 01572 653026).

Our walk starts at the car park and picnic site of Normanton. Then it follows the shoreline via Normanton Tower towards the dam. En route, only 50 yards from your walk, you can divert to Normanton Park Hotel to eat in the stylish bar or on the Courtyard Patio where a wide range of food is on offer. Among the drinks at the bar you will find Ruddles Best Bitter, John Smith's, Courage Directors and Foster's lager. Should you wish for a gourmet meal you can dine in the Lake View Orangery with its selection of home-cooked à la carte dishes. Telephone: 01780 720315.

- **HOW TO GET THERE:** From Stamford and the A1 take either the A606 or the A6121 and follow signs. From Oakham take the A6003 turning left at Manton for Edith Weston.
- **PARKING:** There is ample parking at Normanton Picnic Park. There is a small charge which entitles you to use all the reservoir car parks on that day.
- **LENGTH OF THE WALK:** 3 miles. Map: OS Explorer 15 Rutland Water and Stamford (GR 929056).

THE WALK

1. Start in the Normanton car park. Go east towards the harbour where you see boats moored. In the Tipsy Trout you can get a snack and drink. Go on beyond this either on the track or via a stile and you come to the church - Normanton Tower. This is open from Easter to October daily 11 am to 4 pm.

2. Carry on along the shoreline and soon you see Normanton Park Hotel on your right. The walk then continues along the shore to the dam. As you reach a large tower - the draw off tower - bear right to a metal gate then onto the main road. Turn left and keep to the wide verge for about 300 yards until you see a footpath sign in the trees on the opposite side of the road. Cross to follow this sign.

3. Climb a metal gate into the wood. Here a marker post indicates that you go across the large field diagonally right to a tree in the far corner.

4. Cross the stile into the lane then turn right. Carry on for about ½ mile to a sharp bend. Here a footpath sign shows that you should go through a wooden gate into the field, following a wall which is on your right. Then via a series of three gates you reach another lane near Top Cottages, which you see on your left. This path is entirely straight and the farm you pass on your left is Normanton Lodge Farm, a remnant of the old estate buildings of the Earl of Ancaster.

5. On reaching the lane go over the stile and turn right. Follow the lane for ¾ mile until you arrive at a main road. Here you can cross, climb a fence and return to the car park (this road used to go north but, as you see, the reservoir put an end to that). If you prefer, you can reach the car park by turning left to follow the main road for about 300 yards to the official entrance.

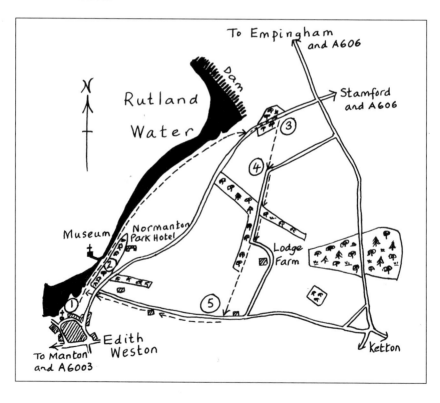

Normanton Park Hotel's attractive courtyard patio

PLACES OF INTEREST NEARBY

Stamford, a historic stone-built town, is just a few miles to the east. *Uppingham*, with its famous public school, bookshops, market square and ochre-coloured buildings, is 5 miles south. *Wing Maze* in the village of Wing, to the south-west, is a modest, yet interesting medieval turf maze which can be viewed free. Nearby *Lyndon* is the former home of Thomas Barker, Father of English Meteorology, who kept records of the weather and the countryside for 60 years in the 18th century. You can see the church where he is buried.

The draw off tower and dam at Rutland Water

EYEBROOK RESERVOIR AND THE GUNPOWDER PLOT

Eyebrook Reservoir, half in Leicestershire and half in Rutland, is a popular trout fishing and bird watching site. Nearby Stockerston and Stoke Dry are small villages with their own particular charm. In the former is the lovely lane leading up to St Peter's church; the latter's charm lies in its cliff-hanging position on the side of the reservoir and the links which can be found with Sir Everard Digby and the Gunpowder Plot. This varied route takes you through both villages and includes a stretch alongside the reservoir.

Eyebrook Reservoir

The walk begins at the church in Stockerston with Stockerston Hall close by. Passing through the tiny village you soon reach the margins of Eyebrook Reservoir which you follow for about a mile before turning away to arrive at Stoke Dry. The reservoir was built between 1937 and 1940 to supply water to the steelworks in Corby. It was one of the places where the famous Dam Busters practised. There are fine views over the whole of Eyebrook during the walk.

St Andrew's church in Stoke Dry has many special features to see. Over the porch is the room where, legend tells us, Sir Everard Digby, executed in 1606 for his part in the Gunpowder Plot, may have met his fellow conspirators. Look for the curious carvings in the church, also 'Red Indians' in the wall-painting depicting the martyrdom of St Edmund. How could this 13th century mural contain Indians with bows and arrows when Columbus had not yet discovered America?

Beyond Stoke Dry you eventually pass through cool woodland for $\frac{1}{2}$ mile and then downhill back into Stockerston. There are no pubs en route but if you wish you can divert to the Old White Hart in Lyddington, which is one mile from Manor Farm north of Stoke Dry. Here you will find a real country pub atmosphere with a small bar, a medium-sized lounge and the Hunters Restaurant. There is a strong emphasis on home-cooked food, for example, sausage and mash, fresh Grimsby haddock in batter and a roast of the day with all the trimmings, as well as vegetarian dishes. Food is available from 12 noon to 2 pm and 7 pm to 10 pm every day (not Sunday evening). This freehouse offers Greene King IPA and Abbot Ale and Marston's Pedigree. Telephone: 01572 821703.

- **HOW TO GET THERE:** From the A47 or A6003 at Uppingham take the B664, Stockerston Road. Alternatively, Stockerston can be reached on the B664 from Medbourne or via minor roads from Great Easton and Stoke Dry.
- **PARKING:** There is a small space to park near the church at Stockerston, also on the grass in the approach lane.
- **LENGTH OF THE WALK:** $4\frac{1}{2}$ miles. Map: OS Explorer 15 Rutland Water and Stamford (GR 835975).

THE WALK

1. Go down Church Lane to the main road. There are views of Eyebrook Reservoir to your right. Turn right at the main road. Go carefully to the bend ($\frac{1}{4}$ mile) and bear left into a narrow country lane. At the sign 'Stoke Dry $1\frac{1}{4}$ miles' turn left, eventually going uphill into Stoke Dry village.

2. There is a seat in the churchyard where you can take a well-deserved rest. Then carry on through the village uphill to Manor Farm on your left. Go left into the bridlepath as indicated, through metal gates with marker posts and alongside the hedge on your left. The shallow depression to your right may be the boundary of the Bishop of Lincoln's Lyddington Deer Park in medieval times.

3. At the far corner of the field go through an open gate onto a track (marker post). Follow the hedge on your left. Continue ahead along the bridlepath (with blue arrows). **Do not** go over a stile on your right.

4. Now cross the field diagonally left to a marker post. The bridlepath continues left through a five-bar gate into a rough grassy path with nettles. There are excellent views of Eyebrook to your left.

5. Carry on with the hedge to your right. Marker posts show the way, round the edge of the field towards the wood (Stoke Dry Wood). As you reach the corner of the wood you find a marker post. Although the post indicates straight on for the bridlepath, you must turn immediately into the wood on your left. Follow the path through, which has a marker post halfway and also plastic ties on some trees to show the track. At the second marker post turn left and continue through the trees.

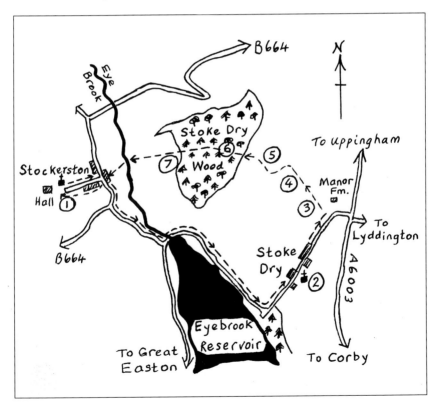

85

6. You will find marker posts to show the path, also more tree ties. You go downhill until you reach a wooden gate into a field. Stockerston and its church can be seen ahead.

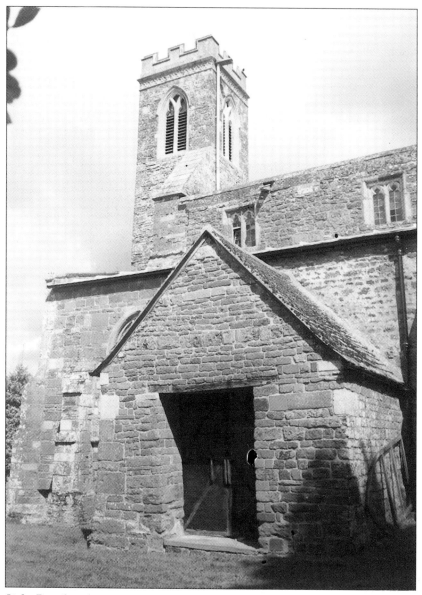

Stoke Dry church

7. Cross the field to the far marker post. Here, climb over the stile and the next one, only a few yards away, cross a footbridge to the left over the tiny Eyebrook river. Then go left diagonally across the field to a metal gate. Pass through this onto the main road. Cross into Church Lane to return to your starting point.

PLACES OF INTEREST NEARBY

There are some lovely villages nearby such as *Medbourne* and *Uppingham* (where tours of the public school can be arranged, telephone: 01572 822672). *Lyddington Bede House*, the former palace of the Bishops of Lincoln, is open daily from April to October (telephone: 01572 822438). The 400-acre trout fishery at *Eyebrook Reservoir* is open from March to October and offers day tickets for bank and boat fishing (telephone: 01536 770264).

The sign to Stockerston village

KETTON: A TWO RIVERS WALK
♨︎

The Welland meanders in a wide floodplain and it separates Rutland from Northamptonshire. A much smaller stream, the Chater, joins the Welland just to the south-west of Stamford. Together with stretches beside both rivers this walk visits the interesting village of Ketton, which takes its name from the Chater, and the adjacent hamlet of Aldgate, linked by Church Road bridge.

The River Welland

Ketton is one of Rutland's larger villages and is located in the extreme east of the county, only a few miles from Stamford and the A1. It is famous for its building stone which has been used in the Tower of London, Buckingham Palace, York Minster and some Cambridge colleges. Since 1929 the large cement works, which dominates the village, has continued to expand. Today, however, there is little left of the old industry except for Ketton Architectural Stone and Masonry in Pit Lane.

The village is a living example of the building craft of long ago, from the exceptional church of St Mary the Virgin, with its fine carved west doorway and its absorbing gravestones executed by local stonemasons, to nearby Garden Cottage, the Vicarage, the Railway Inn and over 100 stone buildings listed as Grade II in a very large Conservation Area.

The Hereward Way and the Jurassic Way converge on Ketton and there are many other walks in the vicinity, notably in the Old Quarry off Pit

Lane which has been designated a Site of Special Scientific Interest (SSSI) by English Nature as it is the largest area of limestone flora and fauna grassland in Rutland.

Our walk today, however, starts at Church Road bridge, dating from the 17th century but restored in 1849 by Robert Hibbins, from a well-known family of stonemasons. It crosses the railway line via Sooty Bridge and continues alongside the River Welland. Then uphill close to a deserted medieval village called Fregthorpe (of which few signs remain) and alongside the Chater back to the village via Sinc Bridge. Whilst the Welland meanders in its wide floodplain, it is noticeable that the Chater has cut a much deeper valley, which especially around the several lakes and weirs, has a most picturesque quality.

The Railway Inn is situated in a very attractive location down Church Street in Ketton but its opening times are limited to after 5.30 pm Monday to Friday and 12 noon to 7 pm on Saturdays and Sundays. Alternatively, you can repair to the friendly Northwick Arms in the High Street. Here there is a large car park and a play area for children. Bar meals are available in the large, attractive lounge at lunchtimes and in the evenings, the specials boards providing plenty of excellent choices. There is also a restaurant. This is a Mansfield house with Dark Smooth Ale, Cask Ale, Riding Bitter and Old Baily, alongside Guinness on draught, Strongbow cider and Stella Artois and Foster's lager. Telephone: 01780 720238.

- **HOW TO GET THERE:** Ketton is about 5 miles west of Stamford, and just west of the A1, on the A6121.
- **PARKING:** There is room for a few cars at the start of the walk, near Church Road bridge. Otherwise, look in village side streets. Do not park in Church Road or the High Street.
- **LENGTH OF THE WALK:** 2 miles. Map: OS Explorer 15 Rutland Water and Stamford (GR 984044).

THE WALK

1. Start south of Church Road bridge in Aldgate. Opposite The Cottage, a retirement home, you will see a footpath sign. Keep to the left along a grass path. Follow the hedge on your left to a house gate then go through the garden to a kissing gate opposite.

2. Now go along a path with a wooden fence on your left. The modern vicarage is on your right. Cross the road to steps opposite then walk between hedges and over the railway footbridge known as Sooty Bridge. Carry on along the narrow path.

3. At a wide track turn left to join a lane, then turn left to follow the lane between houses. Go through an open metal gate (Anglian Water Authority). Look for a marker post to the left of the sewage works and go along a narrow path between the railway embankment and the wire fence. This may be overgrown for about 30 yards.

4. Go over the stile (arrow) into the field with the river on your right and also views of Easton on the Hill. At a yellow marker post ahead, turn left under the railway arch, via a gate.

5. Go uphill on a wide track. **Do not follow the track as it bears left** but carry on ahead uphill with a seat on your left, also the hedge. Go over a stile and metal gate (post) into the field, bearing right downhill to a bridge over the Chater.

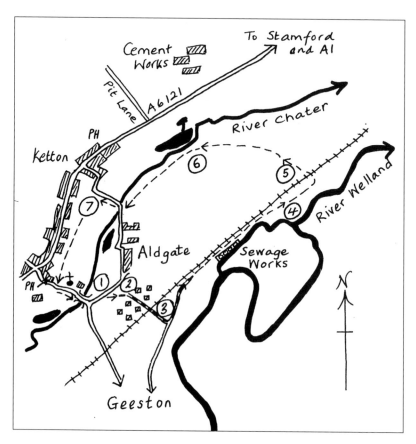

6. Do not cross the bridge but carry on beside the river. **Do not go uphill to your left** but keep alongside the river, over a stile, alongside a fence on your right and through wooden gates. At a sign go right to cross a footbridge (Sinc Bridge) over the Chater.

Ketton church seen across the footbridge

7. Go along the narrow path and in a short distance turn left over a footbridge into the recreation ground. Cross to the far right corner to a marker post to the right of the playground. Continue into the lane which will bring you into Church Street. Turn left towards the bridge and your starting point.

PLACES OF INTEREST NEARBY

Spend some time exploring Ketton itself. In particular, there is a *Geological Trail* in Ketton Old Quarry, Pit Lane, near the modern cement works. A leaflet can be obtained at Ketton Library. To the south-west, *Barrowden*, which has links with Thomas Cook, Father of Tourism, is attractive, clustered around its village pond. *Easton on the Hill* and *Collyweston*, both on the Northamptonshire side of the Welland, are interesting places to visit. The former has a historic *Priest's House*.

TINWELL: A WELLAND WALK

This classic walk through the watermeadows of the River Welland can take you into the lovely historic town of Stamford or you can just return to Tinwell with a glimpse of the spires and towers of the Stamford skyline. The Hereward Way, the Jurassic Way and the Macmillan Way all meet on your route.

The riverside path leading under the A1 bridge

There is a small green in Tinwell, just off the busy main road. Here, a great stone horseshoe frames the Old Forge of 1848. Once this was the post office, as the VR post box indicates, but now it has reverted to its original use as a traditional forge and shop. In front is a well-stone dated 1880. Round the corner is the listed Crown Inn and a nearby notice shows that the Cecil family of Burghley House, Stamford still own much land hereabouts. The church and manor were given to the family at the Dissolution of the Monasteries.

All Saints' has the only saddleback roof in Rutland, which has been dated around 1350. The walk starts in the atmospheric churchyard, crosses to the bridge and then follows the Welland under the A1, past the site of the Stamford Spa, once a medicinal spring, along the Jurassic

Way to Stamford meadows, then retraces the waterside route back to Tinwell. A diversion into Mill Lane brings you to the Crown Inn.

Here you will find a delightful interior with cosy armchairs and a settee. There are seats outside too. Inside there is a small, attractive restaurant. Home-made steak and ale pie, home-cooked ham, eggs and chips, fresh haddock and many appetising snacks feature on the board menu. The wide range of drinks available includes Tetley Bitter, Flowers Original, Murphy's Irish Stout, Caffrey's Irish Ale, Dry Blackthorn cider and Carlsberg lager. Altogether, a most delightful watering hole. Telephone: 01780 762492.

- **HOW TO GET THERE:** Tinwell is close to the A1. It is only 2 miles west of Stamford along the A6121.
- **PARKING:** There is a customer car park at the Crown Inn, (please ask if you want to leave your car while you walk), also room for a few cars on the nearby road as well as opposite the Old Forge.
- **LENGTH OF THE WALK:** 4 miles. Map: OS Explorer 15 Rutland Water and Stamford (GR 006064).

The Old Forge and Shop, Tinwell

THE WALK

1. Start from the metal stile into the churchyard (sign). Cross to the wooden stile opposite. Now aim for the far corner of the field, crossing stiles and going round stables to make for a gate on your left. This brings you to the bridge over the River Welland.

2. Cross the bridge and turn left to follow the riverbank. After you go under the busy A1, take time to look at the restored Stamford Spa, read the plaque and sit for a while. Nearby you will see a weir and the pumping station which extracts water from the Welland and pumps it to Rutland Water. Carry on alongside the river.

3. When you reach an iron footbridge (Broadeng Bridge) cross into the meadows beyond, keeping to the left-hand track towards a house at the far side. You are between two arms of the river. As you reach the house turn right and go down to the main branch of the river.

4. Here, if you wish, you can turn left to follow the river for ½ mile into Stamford. However, for an immediate return journey, turn right, crossing the meadows to the iron bridge. Go across and keep right to follow the river back to Tinwell.

5. On reaching the bridge at Tinwell, cross and turn right along the signposted path which will bring you into Mill Lane. Go to the main road and turn left to return to reach the Crown Inn.

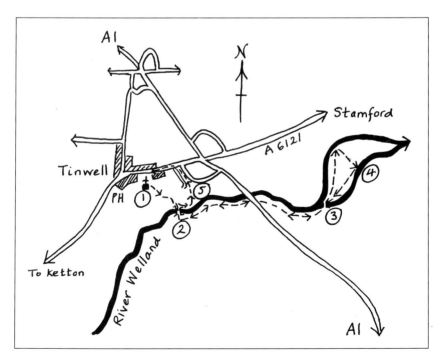

PLACES OF INTEREST NEARBY

Stamford, one of England's finest stone towns, must be the main attraction. For details contact the Tourist Information Centre (telephone: 01780 755611). To the north, at Tolethorpe, is the *Rutland Open Air Theatre* where between June and August, the Stamford Shakespeare Company perform (telephone: 01780 754381). *Burghley House*, south-east of Stamford, is one of England's most magnificent stately homes. Open daily from April to October (telephone: 01780 752451). *Rutland Water* is only 5 miles west of Tinwell with its picnic sites, walks, nature reserve, fishing, sailing, boat trips, cycling, bird watching (see Walks 16 and 17).